Mary Hartley

Heroes

Robert Cormier

Series editor:
Steve Eddy

Philip Allan Updates
Market Place
Deddington
Oxfordshire
OX15 0SE

Orders

Bookpoint Ltd, 130 Milton Park, Abingdon, Oxfordshire, OX14 4SB
tel: 01235 827720
fax: 01235 400454
e-mail: uk.orders@bookpoint.co.uk
Lines are open 9.00 a.m.–5.00 p.m., Monday to Saturday, with a 24-hour message
answering service. You can also order through the Philip Allan Updates website:
www.philipallan.co.uk

ISBN-13: 978-1-84489-611-0
ISBN-10: 1-84489-611-0

Printed by Raithby, Lawrence & Co Ltd, Leicester

Environmental information
The paper on which this title is printed is sourced from managed, sustainable forests.

P00748

Contents

Study and revision

Context

Plot and structure

Characterisation

Themes

Style

Tackling the exam

Answers

Study and revision

Approaching the text

A novel is, above all, a narrative. A large part of the storyteller's art is to make you want to find out what happens next, and therefore to keep you reading on to the end. In order to study *Heroes* and to enjoy it, you need to keep a close track of the events that take place in it. This guide will help you to do that, but you may also benefit from keeping your own notes on the main events and who is involved in them.

However, any novel consists of much more than its events. You need to know the story well to get a good grade in the exam, but if you spend a lot of time in the exam simply retelling the story you will not get a high mark. You also need to keep track of a number of other features.

First, you need to take notice of the setting of the novel — where the events take place — and how this influences the story. You also need to get to know the characters and how Cormier lets us know what they are like. Notice what they say and do, and what other people say about them. Think about why they behave in the way they do — their motives — and what clues the author gives us about this.

As you read on, you will notice themes: the ideas explored by the author in the book. You may find it easier to think about these while not actually reading the book, especially if you discuss them with other people. You should try to become aware of the style of the novel, especially on a second reading. This means how the author tells the story.

All these aspects of the novel are dealt with in this guide. However, you should always try to notice them for yourself. This guide is no substitute for a careful and thoughtful reading of the text.

Using this guide

You may find it useful to read sections of this guide when you need them, rather than reading it from start to finish. For example, you may find it useful to read the Plot and Structure section in conjunction with the novel itself, whether to back up your first reading of it at school or college or to help you revise.

The Tackling the Exam section will be especially useful in the weeks leading up to the exam. Remember to start to revise early — before Christmas for a summer exam.

You are expected to dip into this guide, so you may notice some repetition where topics overlap.

Page references

Page references are given for the Heinemann New Windmill (2001) edition of the text prescribed by AQA.

Context

> What is 'context'?
> How did Cormier's life influence his work?
> What kinds of themes interested Robert Cormier?
> How did the USA become involved in the Second World War?

The 'context' of a novel means the circumstances in which it was written — the social, historical and literary factors that influenced what the author wrote. *Heroes* was written in 1998, but it is set in the period of the Second World War.

Robert Cormier

Robert Cormier was born on 17 January 1925 and died in 2000. He lived his whole life in Leominster, Massachusetts, which became Monument, the setting for some of his novels. The Cormiers' home was in French Hill, the French Canadian area of Leominster, which features as Frenchtown in *Heroes* and some of his other books.

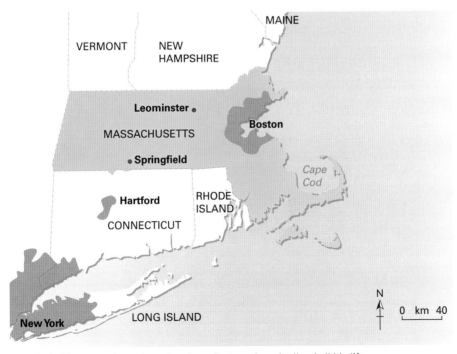

Cormier's 'Monument' was based on Leominster, where he lived all his life

The details about places in the town and the daily life of its inhabitants are based on the real area. In *Heroes*, many local people are employed in the Monument Comb Shop, a factory that produces combs. Comb-making is one of the major businesses in Leominster. Cormier's father was a French Canadian who moved to the area looking for work. He was employed in the comb shop and other factories while he brought up his family.

Robert Cormier attended St Cecilia's School where he was taught by nuns, like Francis and his friends in *Heroes*. He was quite a solitary boy who loved reading and writing, and said that his favourite place as a child was the library. It was one of the nuns who first encouraged him to write, and while he was at college his teacher sent a story he had written to a magazine, which published it and paid a fee.

Cultural influences

Before he became a full-time novelist, Cormier was a newspaper reporter and columnist. The discipline involved in this kind of writing may have helped to shape his style, which is characterised by short dramatic scenes and pared-down language. His style is also influenced by the American writer Ernest Hemingway, whose books Cormier greatly admired. Hemingway used short words and wrote in a direct style.

Cormier loved the cinema. He enjoyed gangster films and Westerns, and was drawn to their depiction of heroes as loners, rebels and outcasts. His love of cinema is reflected in some of his narrative techniques.

Controversy

Although Cormier did not set out to write specifically for a young audience, his books are categorised as suitable for young adults. As this classification indicates, Cormier's work deals with young people and adult themes and ideas. His subject matter is tough — his characters reflect and experience the dark side of the human psyche. They face the existence of evil, betrayal and the corruption of innocence. Cormier's protagonists are teenagers involved in challenging and distressing events. He said that he wanted to 'take real people and put them in extraordinary situations'. He explores with conviction and lack of compromise the emotional conflicts and the moral dilemmas that his characters face, offering no easy happy endings or comforting solutions. In spite of this — or because of it — Cormier's novels draw readers of every generation into gripping, dramatic stories set in a compelling, recognisable world. As one of his teenage admirers said, 'You tell it like it is.'

In the USA, objections can be raised to the inclusion of particular books in public libraries and the school curriculum. The grounds for objection are sexual content, offensive language, religious viewpoint, violence and unsuitability for the age group. A list of 'challenged' books is published annually, and the last week of September every year is known as Banned Books Week. The American Library Association, in association with other academic and literary bodies, makes known the challenges that have taken place in order to stimulate awareness of its belief that people have the right to read material of their choice. Between 1990 and 2004, Cormier was the third most challenged writer; J. K. Rowling, author of the *Harry Potter* books, was fourth; and John Steinbeck, who wrote *Of Mice and Men*, was tenth.

Pause for thought

If you have already read *Heroes*, why do you think it might be seen as offensive or unsuitable?

The USA and the Second World War

The USA joined the Allies in the Second World War in December 1941. On 2 September 1945, Japan surrendered, marking the end of the war.

Pearl Harbor

On 7 December 1941, the Japanese launched a surprise attack on the US fleet based at Pearl Harbor in the Pacific. In this attack, 2,400 Americans died. President Franklin D. Roosevelt referred to the attack as 'a day of infamy', and declared that the USA was at war with Japan. Within a few days, Germany and Italy declared war against the USA. National feeling ran high, and recruiting offices were flooded with Americans signing up to join the armed forces.

TopFoto

The Japanese attack on Pearl Harbor

The Battle of Iwo Jima

In February and March 1945, Japan and the USA fought for control of the Pacific island of Iwo Jima. The Japanese suffered enormous losses during the battle, which was won by US troops. The USA lost 6,821 men in the intense fighting. The battle is famous for the image of American soldiers raising the country's flag at the top of Mount Suribachi, the highest point, during the battle.

Text focus

Look carefully at the opening of Chapter 9 from the start to '...and by train to the headquarters of the marines and navy in Boston' (page 48). Read it several times.

➤ This passage gives us an insight into the circumstances relating to the USA's entry into the Second World War.

➤ Larry's decision to enlist straight away typifies the public's reaction to the attack on Pearl Harbor and the decision to go to war. The mood of the moment was 'Patriotic fever, mixed with rage', a phrase that sums up the feelings of the residents of Frenchtown and the USA as a whole. They were outraged at the attack and fired with the desire to support and defend their country. Cormier refers to the 'sneak attack', illustrating how the surprise element of the offensive added to the country's fury. The expression 'ran rampant through the streets of Frenchtown' creates a vivid picture of feelings running high, and suggests that people are gathering on the streets and in public places to share their outrage and determination to fight.

➤ The way in which Larry announces that he is enlisting reflects his personal feelings and the public spirit. He speaks with 'grim-faced determination' and anger flashes in his eyes. He refers to the millions of others who are taking the same action.

➤ Cormier focuses on how the beginning of war affects the small town. We see fathers and brothers — huge numbers of the male population of Frenchtown — getting on buses in the town square to be taken off to their bases, with everyone gathered to say goodbye. The emotional effect is balanced by the factual details about where each section of the armed forces is based.

Review your learning

(Answers are given on page 81.)

1 Which aspects of Cormier's life are reflected in *Heroes*?

2 What is Banned Books Week?

3 When was the Japanese attack on Pearl Harbor?

4 Who was president of the USA when the war began in 1939 and who was president when it ended?

5 What feelings did the US public experience when Pearl Harbor was attacked?

Plot and structure

> What are the main events in the story?
> How is the narrative structured?
> How does Cormier use flashbacks to unfold the narrative?
> How does the author's choice of narrative form build suspense?

Plot

Chapter 1

* Francis Joseph Cassavant returns to his home town after the war.
* He has horrific facial injuries caused by a grenade blowing up in his face.
* He rents a tenement in Mrs Belander's house.
* He has a gun and a mission to kill Larry LaSalle.

On a cold and rainy day in March, 18-year-old Francis returns to Frenchtown, the French-speaking district of the town in New England where he grew up. He has been in hospital in France and England after suffering terrible injuries during the war. He has lost his ears, teeth and eyebrows, and he has two holes that he calls 'caves' where his nostrils used to be. His cheeks consist of skin from his thighs, which has been grafted on to his face. Francis wears a silk scarf over the lower part of his face, a Red Sox cap pulled down over the upper part, and a bandage over his 'nose'. We learn that in this way he achieves two aims: he hides his injuries and he hides his identity. No one recognises him. Even his voice does not give him away: his larynx has been damaged and his voice is lower and hoarser than it used to be.

Francis takes a third-storey apartment in Mrs Belander's tenement house. She does not recognise him, even though she knew him when he was a young boy who did errands for her, and had baked him a cake on his thirteenth birthday.

He visits St Jude's Church and prays for his fellow hospital patient Enrico, who has lost his legs in the war, for his deceased parents, and for his Uncle Louis,

who gave him a home when he was orphaned. Francis also prays for Nicole, the girl he loves and whom he thinks he may never see again, and for Larry LaSalle. With shocking understatement, Francis tells the reader that he has just prayed for the man he is going to kill.

We learn about Francis's war experiences. He was awarded a Silver Star medal for heroism, but he does not consider himself to be a hero. We also learn a little about his childhood. His mother died when he was six years old, giving birth to a baby boy who also died, and his father died when he was 13. His Uncle Louis gave him a home until he joined the army. Francis was brought up a Catholic, educated by nuns. He actively participated in church services and was an altar boy who helped the priest on the altar at mass at St Jude's Church. The duties of altar boys consisted of bringing the priest the ceremonial artefacts and giving responses to the priests' prayers. The mass and responses were said in Latin, which Francis found difficult.

The Silver Star is presented for gallantry in action

Robert Cormier has chosen to tell the story through the voice of Francis, the first-person narrator. The narrative is told in the present tense and the present time in the book is just after the end of the Second World War. The author intersperses the present-day narrative with flashbacks that reveal important aspects of Francis's previous life. The use of flashbacks helps the reader to build up a gradual picture of the main characters and events. In this chapter, the flashbacks create an understanding of Francis's childhood and experiences in the war. Tension is generated through the slow, controlled release of information that we know will be significant but whose full importance is not revealed immediately. The understated references to Larry and Nicole are powerful and intriguing, and we anticipate learning the whole story.

Chapter 2

* There is a flashback to Francis's childhood.
* We see Francis and Nicole's first meeting and relationship.
* The way of life in Frenchtown is described.
* We learn about Francis's schooldays.

Francis remembers meeting Nicole Renard for the first time. She was a new student at school who arrived in the seventh grade after moving from Albany,

New York. Their eyes met and he fell for her immediately. Francis thought he sensed a connection between them, but Nicole ignored him for some time. Luckily, Nicole became friendly with Marie LaCroix, a neighbour and classmate of Francis, and Nicole's visits to Marie gave him an opportunity to catch glimpses of her.

Francis revealed his feelings for Nicole to Marie, after which Nicole spoke to him using his name. Late one summer evening, she waved to Francis and a group of his friends, causing him to agonise over whether she was actually waving to him or to Joey LeBlanc, one of the group who called out to her.

Francis's narrative reveals details of the way of life in Frenchtown — what the houses were like; the daily routines of the inhabitants; the importance to the town of baseball and their team, the Frenchtown Tigers. We hear more about Francis's schooldays. The nuns were strict. They punished bad behaviour and wrote poor marks on report cards. References to St Jude's Church highlight the importance of religion in Francis's life.

The use of a flashback chapter at this point in the narrative adds to our understanding and knowledge of Francis. The contrast between the past and the present is poignant, as we compare the innocence of those days with the darkness of the present.

Chapter 3

* Francis visits Nicole's old home.
* In a flashback to the war, he describes speaking to a soldier from Frenchtown about Nicole.
* Francis gives Mrs Belander a false name and story about himself.
* He dreams about his wartime experiences. He describes killing two German soldiers.
* He refers to the grenade blowing up in his face.

Now in the present time, Francis goes to the house where Nicole and her parents used to live. He knows she will not be there, but he needs to make this visit. At the window he sees a child's face, which disappears as he smiles at her.

Francis recollects being told that Nicole and her parents had simply disappeared one night. In a flashback section, he describes the time when he heard this news. It was in France during the war, when he and an older boy from Frenchtown, Norman Rocheleau, happened to meet in a village outside Rouen. Norman told Francis that Nicole had become like a hermit, not going out at all, and that the family had left Frenchtown without saying a word. We discover that Francis forged his birth certificate to join the army at the age of 15.

Bombed buildings in Rouen, France, in the Second World War

In the present time of the narrative, Francis gives Mrs Belander a fictional account of his life, including a false name. He goes to bed and dreams of the war. In a mixture of dreams and waking recollection, he describes the French village and the GIs in his platoon. Two of his fellow soldiers died and one was wounded by the artillery shells that bombarded them. Francis recounts how he killed two young German soldiers, and how the next day a grenade blew his face away.

Again, we see the techniques used by Cormier to slowly fill in the details. In the flashback, he reveals how the relationship between Francis and Nicole developed. He fleshes out the story of her departure from Frenchtown, but leaves many questions unanswered. The last sentence of the flashback sequence (page 15) prepares us for the moment when Francis kills someone, but at this point we do not know who it is. Tension is generated at the end of the chapter as Francis anticipates the day when Larry will appear on the streets of Frenchtown.

Pause for thought

Why might Nicole and her family have suddenly disappeared?

Chapter 4

* Francis walks in the direction of the Wreck Centre.
* He meets Arthur Rivier, who buys him a drink in the St Jude Club.
* Francis hears local men reminiscing about their schooldays.
* He decides to visit the Wreck Centre, although he knows that nothing good will come of the visit.

The introduction of the Wreck Centre raises questions in the reader's mind. This seems to be a place associated with whatever it was that happened in the past, and with the 'loneliness and regret' that Francis experienced after visiting Nicole's house.

Arthur Rivier stops Francis as he is on his way to the Wreck Centre — recognising not Francis himself but an injured war veteran — and buys him a drink in the St Jude Club. The meeting with Arthur confirms that Francis's disguise works, and also confirms his status in the eyes of others as a war veteran worthy of sympathy and respect.

Arthur is one of a group of Frenchtown men who enlisted in the armed services, and whom Francis regarded with awe and admiration. Arthur has the added cachet of having been a great baseball player for the Frenchtown Tigers. When these men came home on leave in their uniforms — Arthur with his corporal's stripes — they were role models for Francis. They were heroes fighting for freedom, and he longed to be old enough to join up and be like them. Members of this group are now in the St Jude Club, drinking beer and playing billiards, discussing what they will do now that the war is over, laughing about their schooldays, enjoying a camaraderie from which Francis feels excluded. Again, he refers to not being the hero he seems to be.

At this point in the novel, Cormier offers another view of the effects of war. The men's conversation informs us of the choices available to able-bodied ex-servicemen. The war seems not to have harmed them physically or mentally. In spite of Big Boy Burgeron's bad feet, he is fitter than he was when he joined up. They discuss the possibility of joining the police force or the fire service, and Joe LaFontaine declares he will take advantage of the new GI bill to go to college.

Francis's muffled appearance as he hides his injuries, and his unwillingness to talk, are a pointed contrast to the men's behaviour. He wants to ask about Larry LaSalle and find out when and if he's coming back. The references to Larry build up slowly, increasing the tension and preparing us for a fateful meeting.

Pause for thought

Why does Francis keep saying that he is not a hero? At this point, has he done or said anything to support his view of himself? How does the perception that Francis is a hero help him to maintain his disguised identity?

Chapter 5

- Francis approaches the Wreck Centre.
- He tells the tragic story of why the Centre was closed down.
- He describes how Larry LaSalle reopened the Centre for young people in Frenchtown.
- We learn that Francis used to see Nicole at the Centre.
- He remembers that Joey LeBlanc always felt it was a doomed place.
- He reveals that Joey LeBlanc was killed in the war.

The first thing we notice about the Wreck Centre (formerly known as Grenier's Hall), apart from the fact that it is boarded up and abandoned, is the pun in its name. The faded lettering on the door indicates that its original name was the Frenchtown Recreation Centre, a title shortened to 'Rec.' and turned into 'Wreck' for a joke. The play on words alerts us to the idea that somehow this place is

Fred Astaire and Ginger Rogers

associated with personal and emotional wreckage; that it was perhaps the scene of events which wrecked people's lives. This feeling is emphasised by Francis's recollection that the Centre was a place of bad luck, thought to bring doom.

The hall's reputation was created by a tragic event that occurred there. In its original incarnation, Grenier's Hall was a place where happy events like weddings and holidays were celebrated, but the wedding of Marie-Blanche Touraine put paid to that. At her wedding, her rejected fiancé burst in and shot Marie-Blanche and her new husband, leaving the bride dead and her husband paralysed for life. The gunman then hanged himself. Grenier's Hall was closed down and the abandoned building acquired the reputation of being haunted.

Larry LaSalle turned the hall into a venue for young people's activities. He had been in show business in New York, where it was rumoured that he had got into trouble. Larry was an inspirational leader. The Wreck Centre was where the lonely young Francis found a second home, and where he regularly saw Nicole, who went to dance classes there.

The focus on the Wreck Centre highlights the many ways in which Francis's life has been torn apart. Not only has his face been ruined, but we feel the cumulative effects of devastating occurrences — some that we know about, such as the death of his parents and his injuries, and some that have only been hinted at, which have led him to the point at which the action of the novel begins. The Wreck Centre, with its abiding aura of gloom and bad luck, seems to have been the scene of key events in Francis's life. The reference at the end of the chapter (page 30) to Joey being right — there was doom hanging over the place — creates suspense as we wait for the details to unfold.

Key point

The building that the Wreck Centre is in carries the aura of tragedy and bad luck because of the revenge shooting that took place there. Its reputation as a place haunted by tragedy has become part of Frenchtown folklore. The ideas of love, revenge and ruined lives associated with the Centre foreshadow what is to happen there.

Chapter 6

* Francis has been in Frenchtown for almost a month.
* He watches out for Larry LaSalle and asks about him in the St Jude Club.
* We learn that Larry was awarded the Silver Star in the war.
* Arthur recognises Francis, but respects his wish to remain anonymous.
* We learn that Francis saved the lives of others when he fell on the grenade.
* We learn that Francis was a table tennis champion at the Wreck Club.

Francis has become a familiar figure in Frenchtown. People greet him and smile as he walks the streets, welcoming him as a war veteran. They do not know, of course, that he carries his gun in his duffel bag and that he is watching for Larry LaSalle.

Francis is always made welcome at the St Jude Club, where he joins the group of veterans and listens for any mention of Larry. Eventually, he asks outright if anyone knows when Larry is coming back. The conversation about Larry reveals that he, like Francis, was awarded the Silver Star for heroism in the war. An account of Larry's deeds is in the bartender's scrapbook of Frenchtown soldiers. Francis is in the book as well. Arthur recognises Francis and calls him a hero, but agrees to keep his identity secret.

Although no one knows when Larry is coming back, the sense of inevitability is emphasised with the bartender's observation that 'they all come back to Frenchtown sooner or later' (page 34).

Text focus

Look carefully at the opening of Chapter 6 from the start to '...in case Larry LaSalle should walk in or someone might mention his name' (pages 31–32). Read it several times.

➤ Notice how the present, past and future tenses are seamlessly intertwined. The passage is set in present time, as Francis walks the streets looking for Larry, but he is driven by his memories of the past and his intentions for the future.

➤ The time and place are precisely evoked — it is a rainy early April, nearly a month since Francis arrived back in Frenchtown. The reference to St Jude's Church is a reminder of Francis's childhood. At this point in the narrative, we do not know how the place will feature in future events.

➤ The spirit of the postwar period is created with references to the thriving motor-car industry and the future careers of the ex-servicemen. The feeling of an optimistic future is in contrast to the narrow, grim focus of Francis's own future.

➤ The snapshot picture of Larry, with 'that Fred Astaire strut and that movie-star smile', is a reminder of the past.

➤ We are reminded of the past through the veterans' reminiscences about the old days. Their talk highlights important aspects of Frenchtown life — the church and baseball. The references to the stranger who may have been a major league player in disguise illustrate how shared stories and local folklore draw a community together. We are aware that Francis belongs to this community and shares the same influences — even shares the experience of fighting in war — but is set apart by his own history and personal demons.

Chapter 7

- Francis remembers Larry coaching him at table tennis.
- Larry staged a musical production starring Nicole.
- Larry told Francis that he and Nicole were special to him.
- Larry set up a table tennis tournament and let Francis win.

Larry was aware of Francis's misery and lack of self-esteem, and built up his confidence and self-belief by nurturing and developing Francis's natural talent for table tennis. Francis describes in detail the kinds of moves and techniques that Larry taught him. Francis began to acquire recognition and standing through his prowess at the sport, which became an important activity at the Wreck Centre through Larry's promotion of it.

At the same time, Nicole took the limelight as a stunning dancer, the star of *Follies and Fancies*. Larry and Nicole seemed to have a close relationship. They danced together, and did not seem like teacher and pupil.

The table tennis tournament and the production were to take place on the same weekend. Francis won every game in the competition, and the high point of his victory was not just the success but Nicole's support and endorsement. She told Francis she loved watching him play, and invited him to the after-show party the following night. At the end of the table tennis competition, she presented him with a trophy. In response to the crowd's chanting, Francis and Larry then played against each other. Two games took place — the straightforward match that the crowd saw, and the subtle psychological match in which Larry let Francis win.

This chapter ends on a tense note. As Francis savours winning the tournament and the possibility of winning Nicole the next day, a terse final sentence tells us that the next day was 7 December 1941.

Key point

The table tennis tournament and the final match between Francis and Larry have several layers of meaning. On one level, the descriptions of the games are straightforward accounts of battles of skill, and on another level they have a symbolic value, presenting aspects of the relationships between Larry, Francis and Nicole.

Chapter 8

- As Francis walks the streets at night, he finds Arthur, who is drunk.
- Arthur wants to talk about what the war was really like.
- He says there are no heroes.
- Armand and Joe arrive and look after Arthur.

The narrative switches to the present as Francis continues to walk the streets day and night looking for Larry. He finds Arthur on Third Street, drunk and morose. Arthur wants to talk about the reality of war, about the things no one mentions. He says they weren't heroes, they were just there, and they were scared, homesick boys. Francis tries to support Arthur and stop him sliding down the wall, but he is too heavy for him. Armand and Joe arrive and help Arthur home.

This short chapter is a sombre recollection, placed between the dramatic presentation of the day at the end of Chapter 7 and the account in Chapter 9 of what happened after the declaration of war. Arthur's observations about heroism add resonance to the description of Larry's heroism to come in the next chapter.

Pause for thought

Do you agree with Arthur that the men in the *Frenchtown Warriors* scrapbook were not heroes? Can there be more than one type of hero?

Chapter 9

* The Japanese attacked Pearl Harbor and the USA declared war on Japan.
* The after-show party broke up.
* Larry enlisted and the Wreck Centre was closed.
* The people of Frenchtown adjusted to a different way of life.
* Francis and Nicole started dating.
* Larry was featured in a newsreel as a hero who had saved many lives.

This chapter carries on from the point at which Chapter 7 finishes. We learn that 7 December 1941 was when the Japanese attacked Pearl Harbor and the USA declared war on Japan. The after-show party broke up when the news was announced. Larry and many of the Frenchtown men enlisted immediately, and the Wreck Centre was closed. The life of Frenchtown changed. The kids then hung out in the St Jude's schoolyard or in front of the drug store. The adults also gathered at the drug store to read the newspapers and discuss the progress of the war.

Francis plucked up the courage to ask Nicole to go to the movies with him. They became close, and we see the strength of their friendship as they discuss their plans and ambitions. Nicole supported and encouraged Francis's talent for writing. He responded with, 'Oh, I could never write a book' (page 51), which foreshadows the writing of *Heroes*. Nicole is again linked with the convent, where she went to help the nuns knit items for the armed forces.

The town received the news that Larry had saved the lives of an entire platoon. Everyone flocked to the cinema to see Larry's appearance in the Movietone News.

Following immediately after Arthur's present-day rejection of the concept of heroism, we see Larry being acclaimed for his bravery. The song 'Dancing in the Dark' (a swing tune from the era) links the periods before and after the declaration of war. It is the song that Nicole danced to in the production of *Follies and Fancies*. Here it is a reminder of how their world has changed, and how the party and the show have diminished in importance.

Chapter 10

- Francis recalls his time in England.
- He burns the address and telephone number of Dr Abrams.
- He burns the list of hospitals that Enrico gave him.
- Francis waits for Larry's 'second' homecoming.
- He refers to the first time that Larry came home from the war.

Francis tells us that in the hospital in England he did not wear his scarf or bandage. However, on his visit to London he realised that his appearance shocked and frightened people, and he tried to hide his face. Now his face is partly healing, but its shape and appearance are becoming those of a stranger.

We see his determined focus on his mission to kill Larry, and we realise that Francis sees no future for himself beyond the point of accomplishing this. He burns the details that Dr Abrams gave him, and he burns the list of hospitals that would enable him to find Enrico.

As Francis waits for Larry's homecoming, he tells us that this will be Larry's second return to Frenchtown. His first homecoming had something to do with Nicole, and changed their lives for ever. This dramatic twist in the narrative brings us nearer to the point of understanding what happened and why Francis is determined to kill Larry.

Pause for thought

What did Dr Abrams suggest to Francis in Chapter 1? Why does Francis burn the doctor's details? Why does he burn the information on Enrico's likely whereabouts?

Chapter 11

- Larry came home to Frenchtown on leave.
- He received a hero's welcome from the Mayor and the townspeople.
- There was a huge celebration.
- Larry arranged for the Wreck Centre to be opened for a special night.
- They played music, danced and played table tennis.
- Larry asked Francis to leave so that he could have one last dance alone with Nicole.
- Francis stayed in the foyer and listened to them dancing.
- He heard Larry raping Nicole.

- Nicole, distressed and in tears, stumbled out, and saw Francis.
- She rushed off, and Francis heard Larry leave.

This chapter describes events from Larry's triumphant homecoming to the incident we have been waiting to discover. At last we understand the reason for Francis's hatred of Larry.

Francis describes the hot and humid afternoon in July when the town assembled at the station to greet Larry. Kids from the Wreck Centre and their parents were there, as well as the mayor and city officials, and they cheered Larry as he stepped down from the platform. All the kids crowded round Larry, wanting to get close to him. Larry established a connection with each one in turn, and showed particular affection when he greeted Nicole. Larry accepted the mayor's praise modestly, and referred to all the men and women who were fighting and giving their lives to defend freedom. He publicly declared that he wanted to spend time with the Wreck Centre gang, who were thrilled at this acknowledgement.

We hear about the celebration at the City Hall, the one place in town ablaze with light in those cautious times of war. The group sat in a special section of the balcony before being called down by Larry to the entrance of the hall. He led them in a wild snake dance to the Wreck Centre, which he had arranged to be open. They relived the bright and exciting days of the Wreck Centre, until everyone except Larry, Francis and Nicole had gone home.

The atmosphere changed as Larry told Francis to leave because he wanted to have a last dance with Nicole. We can see that Francis was not sure what was happening. He was caught between his automatic instinct to do what Larry asked and his own desire to stay, to be part of what was going on. Although Nicole asked him not to go, Francis did as Larry requested. He stayed in the hallway, not wanting to leave, thinking that by staying he would be proving that he had done what she wanted and not what Larry had wanted. He heard Nicole and Larry dancing to 'Dancing in the Dark', then the music stopped and he heard the sounds of Larry raping Nicole. The attack is described through brief impressions of sounds.

As Nicole ran out, she saw Francis in the hallway. We feel her shock and disbelief, the dreadful sense of betrayal, as she realised that he had been there all along. Francis is left at the end of the chapter to face himself and the realisation of what he has done.

Key point

The song 'Dancing in the Dark' is associated with Larry's feelings for Nicole. The first time it is played, it is linked with her starring role as a dancer. It acquires sad connotations because it becomes a reminder of how their lives change when war is declared. Finally, the song is the macabre accompaniment to Larry's attack on Nicole.

Chapter 12

- Francis waited outside Nicole's house for three days.
- We hear that Larry suddenly left town.
- Nicole accused Francis of not helping her and told him to go away.
- He hid in the confessional box at St Jude's Church.
- He climbed the steeple and thought of throwing himself off.
- He enlisted in the army.

Francis's guilt and self-loathing are evident from the beginning of the chapter. He describes how he watched and waited for Nicole, but saw no sign of her for three days. In the meantime, Larry had gone, and everyone was wondering why he had suddenly disappeared.

Francis finally saw Nicole. Consumed with a sense of guilt and failure, he faced Nicole's accusation that he had known what was happening and had done nothing to help her. He asked her what he could do, but her anger, contempt and hurt were overwhelming, and she told Francis to go away.

Later in the week, Francis went to St Jude's Church and hid in the confessional box until the building was closed. He climbed the steeple and gazed down at Frenchtown. He thought of jumping off and plunging to the pavement, and started to pray. He was persuaded not to jump by the knowledge that the Church regarded suicide as a sin and by the thought of the disgrace it would bring on his family.

Now we discover why Francis forged his birth certificate so that he could join the army. Unable to bring himself to die such a cowardly death, he set off for war seeking a hero's end.

Chapter 13

- Francis hears that Larry has returned from the war and walks as if he has been injured.
- Francis discovers Larry's address.
- Larry is living in a tenement, painted green, on the corner of Ninth and Spruce Streets.

Back in the present, the way in which Francis discovers Larry's whereabouts is almost an anti-climax. He overhears Mrs Belander and Mrs Agneaux gossiping, and gleans enough information to enable him to find Larry.

This short chapter ends with three short sentences, building up the tension as we prepare for the confrontation that has been waiting at the heart of the narrative.

Chapter 14

* Francis goes to Larry's tenement.
* They shake hands.
* Larry initiates a conversation about heroism and the old days at the Wreck Centre.
* Francis reveals that he fell on the grenade in an attempt to kill himself.
* He confronts Larry with his assault on Nicole.
* Larry shows Francis his own gun and says that he contemplates suicide.
* Larry asks Francis to go.
* Francis does not kill Larry.
* As Francis leaves, he hears a gunshot from Larry's room.

Francis finally comes face to face with Larry. The moment is undramatic, even ordinary. Larry's appearance is different. He is sitting in a rocking chair and appears fragile, lacking the dominance and presence of the past. He does not know what Francis is there for, or that Francis knows what happened at the Wreck Centre. Larry does know about Francis's face and about his Silver Star. He does not shy away from Francis's appearance, seeing it as a symbol of his bravery. He praises Francis's table tennis prowess and Francis is overcome by sadness at the thought of those days and how things have turned out. Francis tells Larry that he was not a hero — he was looking for a chance to die honourably in war.

When Larry asks Francis why he wanted to die, Francis finally confronts Larry with what he did to Nicole. Larry tries to take away the guilt, telling Francis that there was nothing he could have done anyway. The moment has arrived, and Francis takes the gun out of his pocket and aims it at Larry. The knowledge of what he is about to do makes his hand shake, and he can hardly believe things have come to this. Larry reveals his fatal weakness for young girls — the strange, twisted love that he has for them. He shows no fear, and waves his hand almost as if dismissing Francis's gun. He tells Francis that his life has changed irrevocably. As well as the psychological wounds, his legs are badly injured. All he wants is to regain the status he had in Francis's eyes, to be the untarnished hero once again — but it is too late.

Francis tells Larry to pray, uttering the words he has so often rehearsed, but Larry forestalls him, and draws out his own gun. He tells Francis that he often thinks about suicide. He says Francis has already accomplished his mission and asks him to leave.

As Francis pauses at the outside door, he hears the shot which tells us that Larry has killed himself.

Pause for thought

What does Larry mean when he says that Francis had already accomplished his mission? Do you agree with him? What is the one sin that Larry refers to? Is Francis also guilty of one sin that wipes away the good things? Do you agree that one sin cancels the good that has been done?

Chapter 15

 * Francis goes to the convent to ask Sister Mathilde where Nicole is.
 * Sister Mathilde says she is proud of Francis and will pray for him.
 * She tells him that Nicole and her family went back to Albany.
 * Francis tells her that a doctor is going to repair his face.

Francis needs to find Nicole. He remembers Nicole's association with the convent and the nuns, and thinks Sister Mathilde might know what has happened. For a moment, he thinks Nicole may have become a nun, but Sister Mathilde tells him that is not the case, although she is being educated by nuns back in Albany. She reveals that she knew Nicole was unhappy when she said goodbye, but it is clear that Sister Mathilde does not know what went on.

This chapter contrasts with the previous one. The convent is a familiar setting from Francis's childhood, the home of the nuns, a place where Nicole also felt at home. The conversation between Sister Mathilde and Francis touches on concepts of prayer and healing, and her fingers move across her rosary beads as they speak.

Chapter 16

 * Francis visits Nicole at her convent school in Albany.
 * He tells her that he will be having cosmetic surgery on his face.
 * Nicole says she is sorry for blaming him for not doing something to help her that night.
 * Nicole has never told anyone about the rape.
 * She calls Francis a hero and encourages him to write about his experiences.
 * They part, knowing that they will never meet again.

The chapter begins with a description of Nicole. Her appearance has changed, and for a moment Francis does not recognise her. He looks for the old hint of mischief in her eyes, but it is not there. Nicole has been damaged by her experience. Her voice is sharp and brittle, and her bright smile does not reach her eyes. She has kept the details of that dreadful night to herself, and says she is gradually adjusting and getting over it. She tells Francis that she is sorry for blaming him for what happened. She thinks of Francis as belonging to the good times, and remembers their days together with affection.

Francis tells Nicole that he needed to see her to tell her he was sorry. He does not tell her that he wants to see if there is still a chance that they could be together, that she could give him a reason to go on living. However, it is too late for this. There is affection between them, but not love. Francis knows that he lost her a long time ago.

The dialogue shows the awkwardness between them. They make light conversation about the old cowboy movies and some of the harmless aspects of Francis's war experiences, but she is relieved when Francis says he is going.

This meeting has been necessary. Francis needed to tell her again that he was sorry, and he needed to see if there was a future for them. He knows that there is not. Their parting is painful, and he wants their final kiss to last for ever.

Francis has received Nicole's forgiveness. She has removed the burden of guilt. She has also urged him to write about his experiences, and to use this means to find answers to his questions about the nature of heroes and heroism. As the chapter ends, we do not know which path Francis will take.

Key point

Our knowledge and understanding of Francis's situation gradually increase as pieces of information are disclosed. Only in Chapter 16, the penultimate chapter, are all our questions about the past answered.

Chapter 17

* Francis sits in the railway station.
* He thinks about the soldiers he has known.
* He considers that ordinary soldiers were the real heroes.
* He thinks about what he could and should do in the future.

Francis thinks about the men in his old platoon, those who were injured and those who died. He thinks about the Frenchtown men who went to war, 'scared kids' who stuck it out, did their jobs and never talk about what happened. He considers those who received no awards to be the real heroes.

He thinks about starting to write about these men. He thinks of other things he could do — contact Dr Abrams and get his face repaired or find Enrico. We feel the possibility of recovery and a future.

Francis also thinks of the gun in his duffel bag, the 'nice and comfortable' weight on his back. The novel ends on this ambiguous note. The gun is still a welcome presence. However, its weight is now comfortable. This might suggest that Francis is finally at ease with himself. We may also assume that he did get hold of a typewriter and wrote his story.

Pause for thought

In which different ways could the book's ending be interpreted? What do you think it suggests about Francis's future?

Structure

Structure refers to the way in which the author arranges the sequence of events that form the plot. The writer makes choices about where to begin and where to end the story, and about the order of events in the middle. A typical way of structuring a book is to introduce us to the characters and setting at the beginning, dealing with the obstacles and conflicts the characters experience in the middle parts, and presenting a resolution at the end.

Heroes has a complex structure. The story is not told chronologically but through a series of flashbacks. The slow build-up of hints and references give the reader some idea of what has happened, but still leave many questions unanswered. We meet Francis at the beginning of the novel, but at a point in the time sequence when his story is reaching its end. He is introduced in the opening words — 'My name is Francis Joseph Cassavant' — and before the end of the first chapter we know that he intends to kill Larry LaSalle. The structure of the novel places this intention at the forefront, and immediately establishes the central tensions of the story as we wonder how and why this event will happen. The essential background information to Francis's quest is revealed gradually. As we read, we piece together the flashbacks, hints and allusions that lead us towards the centre of the narrative: Francis's motive for murder.

Timeline

The action takes place between about 1940 and 1946, after the Second World War ended.

Year	What happens
1940	Nicole joins the school and Francis falls for her. Larry opens the Wreck Centre
1941	Francis spends his leisure time at the Wreck Centre. Larry is the teenagers' leader and mentor. Francis becomes table tennis champion
7 December 1941	The attack on Pearl Harbor brings the USA into the war
1942–43	The war years continue. Francis and Nicole date
3 July 1943	Larry returns, a war hero. Larry rapes Nicole in the Wreck Centre. Larry leaves

Year	What happens
Around 10 July 1943	Francis wants to kill himself. He forges his birth certificate to join the army (aged 15). Nicole and her family move back to Albany
1943–45	Francis falls on a grenade and is horrifically injured. He is awarded the Silver Star for bravery. He is in hospital in France and England
March–April 1946	Francis returns to Frenchtown, intending to kill Larry. He confronts Larry but does not kill him. Larry shoots himself. Francis finds Nicole. Nicole forgives him. Francis faces the future

Use of flashback

Chapter 1 is a good example of the flashback aspect of Cormier's technique. It reveals significant events in Francis's life, which are not presented chronologically but through descriptions of present events interspersed with memories of and allusions to the past.

Here are the events in the order in which they actually happen:
1   Francis's mother dies.
2   Francis's father dies.
3   Francis goes to live with Uncle Louis.
4   Nicole enters Francis's life.
5   He goes to war and is injured.
6   He keeps his gun.
7   He is hospitalised in France and England.
8   Francis returns to Frenchtown.
9   He rents the attic tenement in Mrs Belander's building.
10 He prays in St Jude's Church.
11 He tells the reader that he intends to kill Larry LaSalle.

However, the information is revealed in the following order:
8   Francis returns to Frenchtown.
5   He goes to war and is injured.
7   He is hospitalised in France and England.
9   He rents the attic tenement in Mrs Belander's building.
6   He keeps his gun.
10 He prays in St Jude's Church.

1   Francis's mother dies.

2   Francis's father dies.

3   Francis goes to live with Uncle Louis.

4   Nicole enters Francis's life.

11   He tells the reader that he intends to kill Larry LaSalle.

The effect of this technique is to build suspense, as crucial information is hinted at but the details withheld. This way of constructing the narrative adds tension and interest as questions are raised but not answered immediately.

Gradual presentation of characters

Our response to the main characters is influenced by the way they are gradually presented, and the way their part in the story emerges as the narrative develops.

Nicole

References to Nicole in Chapter 1 establish how important she is to Francis. Chapter 2 describes their early schooldays and how Francis adored her from afar. The next thing we hear is that she and her family suddenly left Frenchtown. Cormier withholds details of Nicole's departure from Frenchtown, building in hints and snippets of information as the full picture gradually emerges.

In Chapter 3, through Francis's conversation with Norman Rocheleau in the French village, we discover that Nicole did become Francis's girlfriend — he did not carry on adoring her from afar but they kissed and held hands. We also know at this point that for some reason he lost her. We realise that something happened to change Nicole. According to Norman, she became a hermit, hardly ever leaving her house except to go to 'the nuns' mass' (page 15) at 5.30 a.m. Her regular attendance at church at this unsociable hour suggests that she needed to keep away from people, and that she needed spiritual support.

Our questions about what happened to Nicole are not answered until Chapters 11 and 12. These describe the incident that changed the lives of Nicole and Francis for ever, and let us know why he joined the army and wants to kill Larry. We have to wait until Chapter 16 when Francis meets Nicole for the full picture to emerge. This chapter is the resolution of Francis's conflict with Nicole, and paves the way for the short final chapter in which he can face the future with a clear conscience.

Larry

In Chapter 1, we are told that Larry is Francis's enemy, and that Francis intends to kill him. These two facts are at the core of the narrative. In Chapter 5, the

description of Larry and how he opened the Wreck Centre is a surprise and builds tension — what can this attractive man, who is doing so much to help the town, have done to make Francis want to kill him? Hints are woven into the narrative. There are references to Larry's mysterious and somewhat shady past, and the tone of the description suggests something a little suspect about him. In Chapter 6, we learn that he was a war hero, and we are aware that there are gaps in the narrative that we want to be filled. The flashback Chapters 7 and 9 give us this account. We hear more about the Wreck Centre and how Larry went off to fight. Chapter 11 gives the account of his homecoming and his attack on Nicole. At this point in the narrative, one of our questions has been answered — we know what Larry has done and why Francis is waiting for him with a gun.

Chapters 13 and 14 build the resolution of Francis's conflict with Larry, paving the way for the resolution with Nicole in Chapter 16.

Pace and variety

At key moments, the sequence of the narrative is interrupted, a technique that builds tension and suspense. For example, Chapter 7 ends with the indication that everything changed because the next day was 7 December 1941. Chapter 8 does not give the explanation we are waiting for, but takes us back to the present and the conversation between Francis and Arthur about the war. Chapter 9 picks up the story where it was left at the end of Chapter 7 and lets us know the significance of the date and details about the outbreak of war.

Cormier also uses structure to vary the intensity of the narrative. Chapter 14 ends with Larry's death, and he follows this climactic and emotionally harrowing chapter with a gentler narrative — in Chapter 15, Francis visits Sister Mathilde to find out where Nicole is. This chapter acts as a bridge between the two crucial confrontations, the one with Larry in Chapter 14 and the one with Nicole in Chapter 16.

Structure and themes

The way the narrative is structured also affects our interpretation of events and raises questions about them. The reader knows early in the book that Francis loved and lost Nicole, and that Francis looked up to Larry but then embarked on a mission to kill him. However, we don't know the details, so we scrutinise the text for insights into the reality of events. We piece together hints and impose chronology on the story, but — just as appearance and reality are intertwined thematically in the text — as we read the story we are never sure if our judgements and conclusions are accurate. The structure and the narrative viewpoint are closely interlinked, and we are aware that the way the narrative unfolds is controlled by Francis as the narrator and filtered through his eyes.

Review your learning

(Answers are given on page 81.)

1 What is the name of the cinema in Frenchtown?
2 What is the full name of the school?
3 What is the name of Larry's last musical production at the Wreck Centre?
4 In which month does the novel begin, and in which month does it end?
5 Who does Francis live with after his father's death?
6 Which event causes the after-show party to be cut short?
7 Where does Nicole's family move to after leaving Frenchtown?
8 Which chapters are told completely in flashback?
9 In which chapter is the whole truth about what happened at the Wreck Centre revealed?
10 Which chapters do not mention Larry?

Characterisation

> ➤ Who are the characters and what are they like?
> ➤ What are the relationships between the characters?
> ➤ How does Cormier reveal the characters to us?
> ➤ What part do they play in the plot?
> ➤ How do they fit into the book's themes?

Francis Cassavant

Francis is a gentle, bookish boy, who suffered the loss of both his parents at an early age. He is romantic and obsessive, a dutiful young man steeped in the doctrines of his religious upbringing. As the narrative unfolds, we gradually piece together a picture of a complex, multi-layered character.

Growing up

The tone of Francis's narrative is deliberately underplayed, so that events of great significance are related or revealed without drama or emotional intensity. His mother died when he was six years old, giving birth to a baby boy who survived only a few hours, and his father died of a heart attack when Francis was 13 years old. Francis's comment that he felt his father really died with his mother gives us some indication of the misery and sadness in the household during those seven years. We have to read between the lines to imagine the devastating impact on Francis of the deaths of both his parents while he was still young.

Francis does not present the deaths of his parents as a tragedy, and he speaks warmly of his Uncle Louis, who took him in after his father died. Louis gives Francis a home, cooks his meals and gives him a weekly allowance. At supper every evening, he asks Francis to give him an account of the day at school, and he listens attentively to what Francis says. We receive a picture of a home life of quiet affection and routine.

Although Francis refers to hanging out with the other kids, he emerges as a lonely and solitary figure. He goes around with Joey LeBlanc and they often go to the movies together. The two boys have little in common, and Francis is irritated by Joey's habits, such as his constant talking. Francis is annoyed when Joey calls out to Nicole, and he hates it when Joey says that the Wreck Centre is a place of bad luck because for Francis it is the place where he sees Nicole.

It is difficult for Francis to find his place in Frenchtown. He is 'too short and uncoordinated' (page 28) to be good at baseball, the town's passion. He is a timid boy, not one to find his identity in a street corner gang. He loves the movies and reading. His ambition is 'to read every book in the Monument Public Library' (page 51). He is good at writing and won Sister Mathilde's prize for composition. However, these areas of interest and aptitude are not those honoured by his peer group, and he feels he is no good at anything. He hasn't even got the courage to speak to Nicole.

The Wreck Centre provides an answer. Francis is not talented in any of the performance arts, but he responds to Larry's encouragement and joins a callisthenics class. (Callisthenics are exercises designed to produce fitness and strength.) We see his self-consciousness as he takes his place in the back row to avoid drawing attention to himself. With Larry's coaching, he discovers a talent for table tennis, and his victory in the tournament and over Larry brings him accolades he had never dreamt of.

Francis the romantic

Francis responds to romanticism in life and in art. His feelings for Nicole are romantic. He creates a romantic image of the white silk scarf he wears. The whole tone and structure of his narrative reflects the romance of stories, influenced by movies and books that he loves. His ideas of London are based on stories about Jack the Ripper and the Sherlock Holmes detective stories written by Arthur Conan Doyle. From books such as these, and possibly from songs, he expects London to be a place of fog and gloom. He goes to find the fictional Baker Street address where Sherlock Holmes lived, knowing it does not actually exist.

A sense of duty

The influence of Francis's Catholic religion may have brought about his strong sense of duty and obligation. In many ways, he is a dutiful character who obeys the rules. When he was a boy, he ran errands for Mrs Belander. He talks about how strict the nuns were and how quick Sister Perpetua was to smack their hands with a ruler, but he seems to stay out of trouble. He obeys the rules of the Church and took part in its rituals. He was an altar boy, a position that required him to memorise ceremonial responses and movements. Francis says he found it hard to remember the Latin responses. He prays for the souls of the dead, one of the duties of the Catholic faith. He even prays for Larry because it is a duty to pray for your enemies.

Man with a mission

Francis presents his intention to kill Larry as a 'mission'. In the context of what we know about his spiritual background, the word assumes an almost religious intensity. In Chapter 1, he tell us 'I thought of the gun hidden away in my duffel bag and knew that my mission was about to begin' (page 5). In Chapter 3, his

statement 'I have places to visit now that I have returned' (page 13) imparts a sense of urgency and commitment that implies not only obsession but also a kind of moral imperative. The repetition of the word 'mission' is almost like a mantra. At the end of Chapter 3, he refers to having 'a mission to perform' and to being 'able to carry out that mission' (page 20).

It may be that Francis focuses on the wrong mission, and this is why he does not kill Larry. His quest, which he thinks is for revenge, may really be for forgiveness and redemption for his 'sin' in leaving Nicole to her fate.

Francis's relationship with Nicole

Nicole comes into Francis's life in the seventh grade. From the beginning, we see Nicole as the object of his adoration. On their first meeting, he feels there is a connection between them: 'our eyes met and a flash of recognition passed between us, as if we had known each other before' (page 8). It is as if he feels that they are destined for each other. From that moment, she is the girl who has won his undying love: 'It would always be Nicole Renard' (page 7).

His feelings for Nicole are romantic, and from their first meeting he both idealises and idolises her. He describes her physical appearance, her small and slender figure and her shining black hair, almost in terms of awe. To Francis, she is like an ethereal being present in glimpses, in the murmur of a voice, the occasional sound of laughter. He trails after Nicole as she walks home with Marie, longing for her to notice him and at the same time terrified that if she does he will make a fool of himself. When Nicole finally speaks to him and calls him by his name, he suffers agonies as he thinks about the possible interpretations of the encounter. How little he knows of the real Nicole may be seen when he wants to talk to Marie about her, but realises that he has no idea of the kind of person she is, of her likes and interests. What he does know is that he loves her with all his heart, and wants to shout this fact from the rooftops.

We see Francis developing a more realistic approach to Nicole as he gets older. Like the other young people, she goes to the Wreck Centre, and joins a dancing group. This gives Francis an opportunity to watch and be near her. For him, she still has an aura of holiness and an almost unearthly purity. Even her perspiration when she has been dancing is seen as raindrops on the white porcelain of her forehead — yet at the same time it has a 'musky smell' that mingles with her 'sweet fragrance' (page 30). Nicole may be on a pedestal, but she is a real young woman as well, and Francis's emerging sexuality acknowledges this. When he first saw Nicole, she reminded him of St Thérèse, but now she reminds him of the girls 'in certain magazines at Laurier's Drug Store' (page 30). When she says hello to him now, he feels the same connection as he had felt when they first met in the classroom, but is so overwhelmed by her presence that he cannot say her name.

Francis is consumed by his attraction to Nicole, and her presence at the Wreck Centre makes his life there complete. When she admires his table tennis playing and supports him at the tournament, it is like a dream come true. There is a dreamlike quality in Francis's account of Nicole, in the way he is sometimes uncertain of what her responses mean: he is not sure if she is teasing him; he thinks there is a suggestion of promise and of future shared times in the way that she looks at him; he thinks she may have blown him a kiss. The ambiguity reflects Francis's lack of confidence and also an ambiguity in Nicole.

Francis's delight in the fact that Nicole is noticing and encouraging him is shot through with jealousy of her relationship with Larry. When the situation changes with the declaration of war and Larry's departure, some of the tension and complexity of the relationships between the three of them disappears. To Francis's delighted amazement, he finds he is dating Nicole. There is a sweetness and innocence in the description of their Saturday afternoon movie dates — the way they hold hands and kiss, and the way she lets his hand linger for a moment on her sweater. Francis opens up to Nicole, forgetting his shyness as they talk about books, movies and 'a thousand other things' (page 51).

A 1940s movie house

However, this relationship and their lives are blown apart when Larry returns from the war. Francis is secure in his love for Nicole, promising her 'I'll never leave you' (page 60). As he remarks, it is like a love scene from a movie, a romantic declaration of eternal devotion. The reality is that he does leave Nicole alone with Larry, in spite of her pleas to him to stay, because Larry holds more sway over him. The knowledge that he betrayed Nicole so shamefully, his guilt at this sin, is at the core of the novel and precipitates Francis going to war and his mission to kill Larry. The final turning point is his last meeting with Nicole when he receives her forgiveness.

Francis and Larry

Francis's feelings for Larry are revealed gradually. At first, like all the kids, Francis is drawn under Larry's spell. Larry singles him out for special attention, an action that is all the sweeter because Nicole is also of particular interest to Larry.

Through Larry's encouragement, Francis becomes good at table tennis. He is 'spellbound' (page 38) by Larry's declaration that he has the attributes of a natural player. Because of Larry's intervention, Francis not only achieves a position in the group, but, unbelievably, is at the receiving end of applause, cheers and whistles.

His prowess at table tennis also draws praise from Nicole, causing him to feel 'a tide of confidence' (page 40) for the first time in his life. Larry has turned him into a star, even without his final gift to Francis — the championship he bestows upon him by deliberately losing the game. Francis accepts the victory that Larry gives him with gratitude, giving a whispered 'thank you' as Larry presents him to the crowd as the winner.

Key point

The table tennis match between Francis and Larry is like the showdown at the end of a Western film. Although they are not sworn enemies and do not belong to opposing sides, the match between them is a psychological and physical battle that reveals some of the complexity of the relationship between them. By letting Francis win, Larry loses the game but gains control.

The way that Francis feels about Larry is complicated by the relationship each of them has with Nicole. Francis admires Larry, his coach and mentor, and is enormously grateful for what he has done for him. At the same time he is jealous of his closeness with Nicole, but is aware that in a strange way Larry has manoeuvred events to bring Francis and Nicole together.

The language that Francis uses to describe Larry as he recalls this period reveals something of the hatred and contempt that later take the place of admiration. As he describes the way that Larry made table tennis an important sport at the Wreck Centre, he likens it to the way Larry 'lured' unpromising boys and girls into becoming singers and dancers (page 38). The word has sinister connotations, suggesting temptation and enticement. Francis refers to Larry's lighting arrangements for the production: 'Larry LaSalle manipulated a spotlight he had installed especially for her performance' (page 39). Again, the connotations of the word 'manipulate' in this context suggest Francis's later awareness of Larry's actions and motives.

When Francis stands on the church steps after the war, waiting for Larry to show up in Frenchtown, he is watching for 'that Fred Astaire strut and that movie-star smile' (page 31), a phrase that hints at his ambivalent feelings. Another hint is given when, in the St Jude Club, he wonders if Arthur's reference to 'the patron saint of the Wreck Centre' (page 33) is sarcastic.

When Larry returns on leave, his heroic status is confirmed and intensified. Larry the war hero has the same attraction, the same movie-star smile, with something extra, something harder that has come out of his war experience.

When Larry greets the teenagers, Francis mimes serving a table tennis ball and Larry reciprocates. Francis notices Larry and Nicole exchanging their own greetings, but is only aware of how beautiful she looks when she blushes. Francis is caught up in the excitement of the homecoming, of the evening at the Wreck Centre. He is once more drawn under Larry's spell and does not pick up the signals of Nicole's unease and the undercurrents of the situation.

At the end of the evening — when Larry asks Francis to leave him and Nicole alone — Francis does not want to leave because he 'wanted to be a part of them' (page 62). He thinks Larry might want to be alone with Nicole because he has something to tell her, perhaps that he has found a way to make her a star. Francis is used to doing what Larry wants, and Larry gently but firmly puts on the pressure, somehow convincing Francis that he is indeed tired and should go home. When it comes to a choice between doing what Nicole wants and doing what Larry wants, Francis chooses Larry — a decision that haunts him. Francis seems unaware of the potential danger in the situation. When he lingers in the foyer, it is because he feels alone and jealous of Larry dancing with Nicole, not because he thinks Nicole should be protected. When the song ends and he hears what is going on, he knows what is happening. The thought streaks through his mind and then he is face to face with Nicole, distraught and dishevelled. Francis has to face the anger and reflection of his betrayal in her terrible gaze. From this point on, Francis also has to face the knowledge of his own inaction, and the fact that his hero has committed this dreadful assault.

Nicole Renard

Nicole is presented through Francis's eyes, and his descriptions reflect his love for her. At first, she is seen in terms of near-saintly innocence. Her white dress, the 'pale purity of her face' (page 8), her modest demeanour and Francis's association of her with the statue of St Thérèse endow her with a holy aura. In the summer vacation, she strolls in the school grounds with Sister Mathilde. At the same time, Nicole is robustly human, with a 'hint of mischief' in her eyes (page 8), and we see her laughing and giggling with Marie LaCroix.

On the two occasions when she first acknowledges Francis — when she warns him not to fall off the banister (page 11) and when she greets him as she leaves the Wreck Centre (page 30) — Nicole seems to have a strange teasing in her voice. She is friendly, giving a wave to Francis and his group of friends, but she does not respond to the would-be witticism that Joey calls out, and quickens her pace as she walks away, perhaps indicating that she is not comfortable with that kind of boy–girl banter. There is something slightly solitary and aloof about Nicole, it seems. She goes to the Wreck Centre for the dance classes and leaves

when they are over. Francis tells us that Nicole is a good dancer and that she 'instantly caught the attention of Larry LaSalle' (page 30).

Nicole's talent for dancing adds another dimension to her character. She is presented as a saint, a tease, a giggling friend and a reserved girl. According to Sister Mathilde, she is also secretive — and now she is Larry's dance partner. In a description charged with sexuality, we see them dancing, her face almost touching his, their lips almost meeting, her body slipping down against his. As she lies at Larry's feet, with his eyes looking deeply into hers, we see not only a classic finale to a dance routine but an image of Nicole as a victim who has been conquered (page 39).

She goes along with Larry's construction of the Wreck Centre as a show-business arena. She sees herself as the star Larry has made her, the one whose duty it is to host an after-show party because 'Larry says that's what people in show business do' (page 40). She refers to him as 'Larry', an indication of the closeness and particular nature of their relationship.

Nicole becomes aware of Francis as she watches him play table tennis. She likens his playing to dancing, and says that she loves watching the way he moves and the way he hits the ball. Perhaps we are to think that she is influenced by the fact that Francis is, like her, one of Larry's special protégés. When Francis wins the championship, Nicole seems delighted and exhilarated by his success, and when Francis beats Larry, Nicole claims him as her champion. There is promise in her whispered 'See you tomorrow' (page 45). Nicole emerges as a beguiling character, focusing on Francis in an unexpected way. When she watches the table tennis match between Francis and Larry, it is as if she is watching two suitors fighting for her hand.

As Nicole and Francis begin dating, we discover that she enjoys books and movies, and that she has hopes and ambitions for the future, perhaps in the 'big world out there' (page 51) beyond Frenchtown. She encourages Francis to develop his talent for writing and is able to tease him out of his shyness. Nicole seems to understand Francis and believe in him.

Pause for thought

What do you think of Nicole by the end of Chapter 7? Is she artless and innocent? Why do you think she suddenly supports Francis and roots for him to win the match?

Key point

Remember that we know about all the characters only through Francis's perception of them. We have no insight into Nicole's feelings other than what Francis observes, and his observations are coloured by his own feelings.

When war is declared, Nicole develops a more serious persona, leaving behind the stage-struck period and its values. Larry has gone to fight, and without his attention her dreams of being a ballerina seem to have been forgotten. She says she would like to help the war effort, maybe by becoming a nurse. She spends time with the nuns in the convent, knitting socks and scarves for the troops, and then becomes a volunteer with the Monument Red Cross. When she moves away and is at the convent of the Sisters of the Holy Spirit, she speaks dismissively of nuns and their way of education: 'Nuns are nuns, of course, but at least they don't use rulers for discipline here' (page 84).

Like all the townsfolk, she welcomes Larry home, but she seems to be wary of him. At the celebration for Larry's triumphant return, she asks Francis to 'Stay close to me' (page 60), almost as if she feels the need for protection. When Francis says he is leaving Larry and Nicole to have a last dance together, she is unsettled. Francis cannot read her expression as she asks him to stay, but then she unmistakeably says 'Don't go' (page 62).

Nicole is brutally betrayed — by Larry, her teacher and mentor, and by Francis, her friend. Filled with pain, anger and hurt, she tells Francis to go away. Nicole's pain remains with her for a long time after the rape. She withdraws from society and lives almost like a hermit. She speaks to no one about what happened, but tells her parents she wants to move from Frenchtown.

In her new home and at the new convent school, over the course of three years Nicole begins to adjust. Eventually she can bear to read Marie's letters and think about her times in Frenchtown. She begins to find out 'what I am, who I really am' (page 85). Francis's visit gives her the opportunity to tell him she is sorry for blaming him for not helping her. Nicole's forgiveness of Francis is part of her healing process.

> **Pause for thought**
>
> Who do you think betrayed Nicole more — Larry or Francis?

Larry LaSalle

Larry is introduced as the person whom Francis intends to kill. In the first four chapters of the book, as Francis repeatedly declares his mission to kill Larry, this is all we know about him — that he is Francis's enemy, that he has done something to create in Francis the determination to commit a terrible deed he knows is sinful.

Our first picture of Larry is unexpected. He appears on the day that the Wreck Centre opens, and addresses the crowd of local kids gathered in front of the building. He seems to come from nowhere. He is a tall slim man, with 'a lock of blond hair tumbling over his forehead, a smile that revealed dazzling movie-star teeth' (page 27). This picture is attractive and appealing, and Larry's charisma is shown in the way the crowd bursts into applause. However, Cormier's language alerts us to something a little disturbing about Larry. There is a knowing

self-consciousness about the carelessly tumbling lock of hair, and the movie-star reference suggests artifice and deception.

The description of Larry's physique indicates the areas in which he is extraordinarily talented. He has 'the broad shoulders of an athlete and the narrow hips of a dancer' (page 27). He is a good baseball player, hitting home runs with ease, and he leads the kids through 'vigorous exercises and callisthenics' (page 27). He is also a great dancer. His feet seem hardly to touch the floor as he walks, and he tap-dances with 'machine-gun speed' (page 27). His walk is reminiscent of Fred Astaire.

Larry is also a teacher. His success in sport and athletics, and his shining abilities in the performing arts, seem not to be for self-glorification. He leads classes, brings out the best in his students, and reveals talents they did not know they had. He coaches Butch Bartoneau, the school bully, for a singing part in the Centre's musical production, and elicits from Butch a performance that moves the audience to tears. Larry has a similar success with Edna Beauchene, a 'tall and gawky and shy' girl (page 29), giving her a part that makes her the star of the show. Larry believes all the young people he deals with have potential: 'You are all stars' (page 29).

These successes illustrate Larry's gifts as a leader and a teacher. He has belief in the pupils he coaches, and guides them with patient dedication. He seems to be tirelessly active, always in the Wreck Centre, leading classes, producing musicals, demonstrating arts and crafts. His talent and his energy are dazzling, causing him to be an object of admiration and adulation.

He takes a particular interest in Francis. He shows sensitivity towards the boy's feelings, recognising his self-consciousness and letting him stay in the back row of the callisthenics class instead of calling him to the front to be with the others of the same height. He notices that Francis seems unhappy and lacking in self-confidence, and goes out of his way to build up his self-esteem. He praises his abilities in the callisthenics class, and steers him towards table tennis, saying it will be just the sport for him. Larry turns table tennis into an important sport so that Francis's success has value. The attention and encouragement Larry gives him enable Francis to blossom into a skilled player, a champion. He builds Francis up into an expert, giving him extra lessons, playing countless games against him, teaching him techniques that will make him a winner.

Larry's motives for deliberately losing the match with Francis are ambiguous. He does it well, cleverly just missing shots and feigning frustration, and protects Francis from the public humiliation of defeat or a false victory. He hands the game to Francis as a gift, but it is a gift for which Francis will pay.

Pause for thought

What do you think of Larry's support for the kids and the Wreck Centre? Is there anything in it for him? Does it matter if there is?

The unease generated by the first description of Larry is always present. Although his origins are reassuringly familiar — he was born in Frenchtown, and took dance lessons there, winning a talent contest when he was nine or ten — the rest of his life is shrouded in mystery. There are rumours about his past, about how he had been a nightclub performer in New York and Chicago. These rumours are supported by a faded newspaper clipping someone finds, showing Larry in a tuxedo beside a nightclub placard proclaiming 'Starring Larry LaSalle', but he neither talks about the past nor answers questions. He is said to have 'gotten into trouble' in New York City (page 29), but no one is bothered by these rumours. If anything, the air of mystery adds to his glamour.

Larry's relationship with Nicole generates unease from the beginning. There is something slightly alarming about the way she catches his eye immediately, and the way he turns her into something more than a talented dancer in a youth production. There is underlying sexuality in their relationship, seen in the way they dance together. Larry creates a show-business arena at the Wreck Centre, installing a stage and spotlights. He talks about youth productions in show-business terms and makes Nicole the star of the show, both literally and figuratively.

Yet Larry's persona changes overnight. One minute he is the sophisticated performer with the movie-star smile, the next minute he is a war hero. With a grim and determined expression, he announces his intention to enlist a few hours after war has been declared. He does not welcome praise for his action, declaring he is just doing the same as 'millions of others' (page 48). The next picture we have of Larry is in the Movietone News, appearing 'unshaven, gaunt and drawn, eyes sunk deep into their sockets' (page 53). He has saved the lives of a whole platoon of men, and is 'one of the great heroes of Pacific action' (page 53). When he returns on leave, he has become a fighting marine, with something 'sharper' and 'lethal' (page 58) about his appearance, his body lean and hard.

However, he is still the same Larry. When he returns from war, his charismatic presence is demonstrated by his generosity in providing a celebration for the teenagers at the Wreck Centre, by the connection he establishes with them all individually, and by the easy, unassuming way he wears his heroism. He was their hero before he left, and he is their war hero now. Only Nicole and Francis will come to know the dreadful aspect of Larry's dark side.

There are suggestions that Larry plans his attack on Nicole the moment that he sees her in the welcoming crowd. Francis notices 'the rush of affection on his face' (page 58) — his perception that Larry's feelings for Nicole are of 'affection' showing his own innocence. The contrast between Francis's innocent relish of this special evening and Larry's sinister arousal — 'His face was flushed and his eyes shone with excitement' (page 62) — emphasises the cruel and callous nature of Larry's intention. He uses his power and techniques of persuasion to manipulate

the situation, placing an arm around Francis's shoulder as he tells him to go, putting an arm around Nicole and drawing her to him as he claims his 'last dance'. As Larry leaves the hall after the rape, he whistles the tune of 'Dancing in the Dark'. This chilling detail illustrates Larry's inability to recognise the enormity of his action.

Larry's lust for 'sweet young things' (page 76), which is his terrible fatal flaw, is the secret he carries with him. It may be why he had to leave New York City. This is a part of himself that Larry will not fight and for which he shows no repentance. He accepts the evil, he loves his sin and those who make him sin. When Francis confronts Larry, Larry shows no regret for what he did to Nicole. His biggest regret seems to be that he has lost his status as a hero and that Francis will never again look at him with admiration as he used to at the Wreck Centre. His life as he knew it is over. His leg injuries mean he will never dance again, and he is psychologically damaged and worn out by the war.

Larry's last action before killing himself is to try to make things better for Francis. He offers the comforting thought that Francis's instincts would have led him to fall on the grenade anyway, a gesture that recalls his habitual behaviour of building people up, believing in the best about them. His final gift to Francis is to tell him that his mission is accomplished anyway, which seems to prevent Francis from shooting him.

Pause for thought

What is your final judgement of Larry?

Text focus

Look at the contrast in the presentation of Larry before and after the war. The differences in his physical appearance highlight the ways he has changed, and at the same time remind us how his compelling physical presence was part of what enabled him to gain and abuse his power.

- After the war, his voice is 'a bit feeble now' (page 72). Larry's voice was a powerful instrument — he used it to persuade and motivate. He used it to speak movingly of the Wreck Centre kids and their future (page 59), even while (possibly) planning an act that would blight the future of two of them.
- Until Larry's return after the end of the war, he has been characterised as a dancer and an athlete. The repeated references to Fred Astaire emphasise his nimble and graceful movements. In Chapter 14, we are told 'He rises slowly from the chair, steadying the rocker as he lifts himself up' (page 73). There is an aluminium crutch leaning against the table. Larry's physical strength and appeal, which dazzled his followers and hid his inner corruption, have gone.

Enrico Rucelli

Enrico is clever and worldly wise. He is perceptive and intuitive, and understands love. He knows that 'It's still Nicole' (page 7) for Francis. Enrico gives Francis advice: 'I remembered what Enrico Rucelli in the last hospital had said about how money talks and I began to draw out my wallet…' (page 3).

Enrico bribes a male nurse to bring him and Francis a few bottles of beer. He advises Francis on how to forget Nicole, and accompanies his cynical comment that being a war hero makes men attractive to girls with the bitter near-joke about Francis needing to find a blind girl to love him. All Enrico's jokes have a bitter edge to them. He ironically thanks Christ that he's right-handed because it is his left arm that was blown off. We hardly need Francis's observation that Enrico is not really thanking Christ.

Enrico shows determination in the way he adapts to the loss of his legs and an arm, as can be seen in the way that he learns to shuffle cards with one hand. Enrico talks a lot, holding forth on any topic. Possibly he talks to hide his pain, which is always present. Even when he jokes, his eyes are full of pain, and he gets agonising sensations from the legs that are no longer there. Enrico is planning to kill himself. He tells Francis that he will stay in hospital until he finds 'the proper method of disposal' (page 55).

Marie LaCroix

Through Marie we see Francis's capacity for easy-going friendship. Although convention dictates that boys and girls of that age do not communicate, the two are neighbours and have a comfortable relationship in which they can 'talk about everything and nothing' (page 10). Francis reveals his feelings for Nicole to Marie, but he does not know if she will keep his secret. We never know if Marie told Nicole or not, and if Nicole finally speaks to Francis as a result of anything Marie said to her.

Marie is presented as a contrast to Nicole. She can be earthy and vulgar. She likes to tell jokes and does imitations of Sister Mathilde burping and farting.

The nuns

Francis was taught by the nuns for eight years, and they had a strong influence on his development. Their strict regime was accepted by the school students. We hear that everyone was eager to keep in their good books. Joey used to be punished for speaking out of turn, and when the men are adult war veterans, they joke about the way the nuns kept them in check.

Sister Gertrude is the third-grade teacher. She presents Francis with the scriptural doctrine to love your enemies, a code that has remained with him, creating a moral dilemma for him with reference to Larry.

Sister Perpetua, the sixth-grade teacher, is infamous for her quick hand with the ruler. She seems to inflict punishment for the slightest violation of the rules.

Sister Mathilde is the seventh-grade teacher. She encourages Francis's writing by awarding him the medal for composition. She shows concern and compassion for Nicole and Francis. She is worried that Nicole is unhappy when she leaves Frenchtown, and we see the continued closeness between them in the fact that Nicole writes to her.

Sister Martha, the eighth-grade teacher, is known for doling out physical punishment. She is 'No bigger than a peanut' (page 23), but even at an advanced age she knocks around the big boys in her class.

Mrs Belander

Mrs Belander is generous and thoughtful. She paid Francis well when he ran errands for her as a boy, thereby funding his visits to the cinema, and she baked him a cake for his thirteenth birthday. This would have been around the time of Francis's father's death, so we might conclude that she was showing her sympathy for the orphaned boy.

She is the landlady of her building and is an experienced businesswoman. When Francis arrives, she is quick to pick up the fact that he knows her name, and she holds out her hand for a month's rent in advance. She takes care of her property. Francis's apartment is in good order and very clean. Although the stove in the kitchen only heats a small area, it is polished and looked after. She is a considerate landlady, making Francis soup and giving him extra blankets.

Joey LeBlanc

Snippets of information about Joey are scattered throughout the book. He is the friend who calls out to Nicole, showing off a bit, trying to be funny, and who for a moment is seen as a possible rival for Nicole's attention. On that occasion Francis tells him 'You've got a big mouth' (page 12), and we hear later that Joey 'was often punished by the nuns for talking out of turn' (page 27).

When he goes to see films with Francis, he talks all the way through, keeping up a steady commentary 'like a radio announcer describing the action' (page 28). When Joey says he can feel the old doom hanging over the Wreck Centre, Francis says 'You talk too much' (page 30). Joey may have been saying this for effect. He likes to get attention by being the one in the know. He asks 'Is that his real name?' (page 27) when Larry LaSalle introduces himself. He delights in repeating, 'with raised eyebrows and a knowing look' (page 29), the rumours that Larry had been in trouble in New York City.

Joey may speak out of turn, but his comments sometimes have the ring of truth. What he says about Larry indicates that Larry may not be all that he seems. When Butch Bartoneau gives a moving performance in the Wreck Centre's musical production, Joey observes that he is still a bully. Joey's realism contrasts with Francis's romanticism.

The revelation that Joey died on a beach on Iwo Jima in the South Pacific, which is given with Francis's characteristic attention to detail, adds to the examples of the loss and waste of life caused by the war.

Louis Cassavant

Francis's Uncle Louis demonstrates some of the values Francis honours. He is a man of duty and integrity, who gives a home to his orphaned nephew and treats him well. Louis's life follows a routine. He drinks the same number of beers each evening, listens to the radio, and goes to bed at 11 p.m. Louis does not say much, but he listens to Francis, and Francis is sure of his affection. His habit of not saying much contrasts with those of Joey, whose constant chatter annoys Francis.

War veterans

Arthur Rivier, Big Boy Burgeron, Armand Telliere, Joe LaFontaine and George Richelieu are minor characters in the novel. Through this group, Cormier presents a picture of war veterans who provide a contrast to Francis. As well as contributing to the themes of the novel, they give us insight into the sociological background of the USA immediately after the war. They have nothing to hide — they served their time and emerged from their war experiences with some robustness.

In the aftermath of the war, they appear to have more opportunities than before. There is provision for veterans to get free college education and they are encouraged to take jobs in the public sector. Joe LaFontaine, who did not even graduate from high school, plans to go to college and become a teacher. Armand Telliere plans to become a police officer, and sees riding in a patrol car as preferable to the manual work he did before. Their talk reveals a time of new prosperity, with the Detroit factories producing new Chevrolets and Fords, and a time of new freedom, of release from the protocol of life in uniform.

However, there are moments when their reminiscing of the times before the war dies away. Reminders of what these men went through are seen in the way that Arthur's mouth twitches and Armand stares into space at some remembered horror, and the reference to 'George Richelieu tugging at his pinned-up sleeve which should hold his arm but his arm is buried somewhere in the South Pacific' (page 32).

Through Arthur we receive more insight into the idea of heroism as he declares that they were not heroes in the war — that he and the others like him were just 'scared and homesick' (page 47) boys from Frenchtown.

Dr Abrams

Dr Abrams is the surgeon who treats Francis's injuries. He is encouraging to Francis, telling him that he will heal in time. He has a sense of humour, which he tries to get Francis to develop as well. He tells Francis to contact him in Kansas City after the war is over, when he will be able to perform cosmetic surgery on Francis's face.

When Francis destroys Dr Abrams's address and telephone number, he is not looking to the future at all. However, at the end of the book Francis thinks about trying to find the doctor. Through Dr Abrams, we gain insight into Francis's state of mind and the process of him healing, both physically and mentally.

Review your learning

(Answers are given on page 81.)

1 Who do the following phrases describe?
   a 'the pale purity of her face'
   b 'the broad shoulders of an athlete and the narrow hips of a dancer'
   c 'he was tall and looked like Abraham Lincoln'
   d 'his hair is sparse and grey but his eyes are clear and watchful'
   e 'no bigger than a peanut and she still knocks them around'
2 Who makes the following statements and to whom?
   a 'You are all stars.'
   b 'You deserve a good drink.'
   c 'I love to watch you dance.'
   d 'Am I supposed to feel bad for you?'
3 Why does Francis decide against throwing himself off the church steeple?
4 Which movie star is Larry compared to?

Themes

> What is a theme?
> What are the main themes of *Heroes*?
> How do these themes relate to each other?
> How do these themes relate to the characters?

A theme in a novel is an idea or group of ideas that the author explores. There are several ways of defining the themes in a novel, and in any interpretation of literary themes there is bound to be some overlap. The major themes in *Heroes* overlap and illuminate each other.

Heroism

The title of the novel indicates that heroes and ideas of heroism are among its main themes. Cormier asks us to consider the fact that while there may be false heroes, there are also genuine heroes whose actions deserve commendation.

Heroism and war

One of the central contradictions is the fact that Francis is seen as a hero, as a veteran of the war who has not only suffered horrific injuries in performing his duties but has even been awarded the Silver Star medal for bravery. His disguise — intended to conceal his features — does hide his face, but it also draws constant attention to his disfigurement. He is acknowledged to have earned the right to be honoured, to have drinks bought for him, to have his desire not to talk or communicate accepted. Yet Francis tells us insistently that he is not the hero he seems.

It is assumed that he forged his birth certificate because he was desperate to go to war to defeat the Japanese and the Germans, to become one of that heroic band of men who fought for their country, and that he fell on the grenade to save others. Only Francis knows the truth, or his own version of the truth. When he returns home, he does not want his 'heroism' to be acknowledged.

Larry, on the other hand, is an acclaimed hero. He has also received the Silver Star, and he is 'the best of the best' (page 33), the dancer-turned-hero. He captured the enemy and saved fellow marines. The veterans drink a toast to him and honour his gallantry. In their eyes, Larry truly is the local hero. While Francis hides his face, Larry's is on the silver screen.

The novel challenges the concept of heroism in war. Arthur states 'We weren't heroes' (page 47) and insists he and the others he fought with were just scared kids who happened to be fighting in a war. Yet, at the same time, Arthur and his fellow soldiers are part of the structure and system that turns men into heroes. He admires Francis because he has the Silver Star: 'You're a goddam hero' (page 34).

Heroism is celebrated in the scrapbook of *Frenchtown Warriors* kept by the Strangler, the bartender at the St Jude Club. This book features both Francis and Larry. The status afforded to those who are extraordinarily gallant and who risk their lives to save others is seen in the dignity and formality with which the bartender proposes a toast 'To the Silver Star and the men who wear it' (page 33).

Flawed heroes

Both Francis and Larry are flawed heroes. Larry asks if his one sin wipes away all the good things. Although Francis says he should ask Nicole that, the question remains unanswered. Larry says 'Everybody sins' (page 76), a concept with which Francis is familiar.

Francis himself performed a heroic act for a selfish purpose when he fell on the grenade. He saw a chance to end his life, and men's lives were saved as a result.

Childhood heroes

For the youngsters growing up in Frenchtown, to be a hero you had to excel at something that had significance for your peer group. Being good at baseball gave you status, as did being a gang member. Adults gained heroic status in similar ways — Arthur is something of a hero even before he enlists because he is the star first baseman for the Frenchtown Tigers.

Unsung heroes

At the end of the novel, Francis acknowledges the real heroes, those who stayed and fought, who may not have received accolades, but whose actions were heroic. The men in his platoon, and Arthur and his comrades, are the real heroes.

Pause for thought

Who do you think are the real heroes in the book?

War

The effect of war is presented with brutal, dramatic impact in the novel's opening pages. The descriptions of the injuries suffered by Francis and Enrico are given with unsparing detail, made all the more horrific by the understated tone of the narrative voice. Francis's experiences in the war have given him membership of two new groups. Before he joined the army, he was a schoolboy. Now he is one of an elite group of servicemen, and, in spite of his objection to the phrase, one of the 'heroes' who received awards for bravery. He has now become a 'veteran', a term used to describe former members of the armed forces. This title carries connotations of the honour associated with fighting for one's country, and also of the human sacrifices this entails.

In Chapter 3, Francis's encounter with Norman Rocheleau offers a contrast between life before and after the war, before Francis's appearance changed, a time when he could say 'And I had not yet killed anybody' (page 15). At this stage, Francis is still in some ways the young boy from St Jude's Parochial School. The picture of Francis and Norman sitting on the steps of a bombed-out farmhouse in France talking about Sister Perpetua and the ruler with which she inflicted punishments highlights Francis's comparative innocence in war at this point. He has not yet received the injuries that will make the pain of being struck with a ruler insignificant.

When Norman leaves, there is a jokey embarrassment in their farewells — they cannot see themselves as real soldiers: they are 'two Frenchtown boys in uniform' (page 15). This idea is reinforced by Mr Laurier in Chapter 9, when he points out that the troops fighting on their behalf are high-school students: 'A kid graduates from high school, gets six weeks of basic training with guns and grenades, then overseas he goes on a troop-ship and five months later…he's fighting the Japs or the Germans' (page 52). The reality of war hits almost immediately as, shortly after his meeting with Norman, Francis kills two young German soldiers: 'boys with apple cheeks' (page 19), 'kids like me' (page 75).

The novel presents the idea that there are two wars. There is the glamorous enterprise of drama and heroism, of selfless acts performed in the name of freedom: 'Everyone wanted to go to war in those days to defeat the Japs and the Germans' (page 15). Then there is what Arthur calls 'The war nobody wants to talk about' (page 46). This is the war of fear and nervousness, in which the soldiers were scared and homesick. They vomited, had stomach cramps and diarrhoea. They were not heroes or men with a noble purpose. As Arthur says 'We were only there' (page 47).

Action in the war is presented in sharp detail, cinematic in its effect. Francis's image of Larry as a fighting marine is written in short phrases, like cartoons or film images:

> I remembered how hard it had been to think of him as a fighting marine when he announced his enlistment, but seeing his lean hard body now I could picture him storming a hillside on Guadalcanal, rifle in hand, bayonet fixed, grenades dangling from his belt, pumping bullets into the enemy. (page 58)

From the references in Francis's narrative, we can build a picture of certain aspects of the USA's involvement in the Second World War. The USA entered the war when the Japanese attacked Pearl Harbor, an event that occurred on the same day as the Wreck Centre production and party.

US marines in action, Guadalcanal, 1942

We see the impact of the war on Frenchtown and its inhabitants. As able-bodied men — and many women — of the right age rushed to enlist, the streets were suddenly empty of young males. Roles shifted as youngsters and women took over the jobs that had been vacated. Mr Laurier hired Francis to work in the drug store. The factories went into operation 24 hours a day to produce the everyday items the troops needed. Although an air attack on Monument was unlikely, wardens patrolled vigilantly and the town followed blackout procedures. There were the rumours typical of war-time, talk of the sightings of U-boats and disguised Nazis.

. Joey LeBlanc died at Iwo Jima, which tells us that Joey joined the marines and took part in the invasion of the Japanese island. He was one of the 23,000 casualties out of the 70,000 marines who took part.

Love

Francis's feelings for Nicole capture the pain of young love — the doubts and insecurities, the hopeless yearning after someone who barely acknowledges your existence. He worships Nicole from afar, happy to trail behind her as she walks home with Marie, longing for a chance to catch her attention, to hear her mention his name. We feel his self-conscious awkwardness as he does not trust himself to keep his voice steady should he ever pluck up the courage to speak to her. When Nicole does eventually speak to Francis, he is consumed by doubt and embarrassment, and scrutinises every aspect of the fleeting instance for its possible implications.

The account of the meeting between Francis and Norman Rocheleau in France is the first indication we have that the relationship between Francis and Nicole did blossom. Norman asks 'Didn't you go out with her for a while?' (page 14), and the casual, colloquial expression is a contrast to the intensity of Francis's feelings. The memories that overwhelm Francis give us brief snapshots of his time with Nicole — a kiss, her hand in his as they walk along the road, the smell of her perfume. As the details of their relationship gradually unfold, we receive a picture of innocent, traditional teenage dating. Francis eventually plucks up the courage to ask Nicole out, and we see them holding hands in the movies, experiencing their first tentative kiss, talking about their dreams and ambitions, and 'a thousand other things' (page 51). Moments of awkwardness are realistically described as they take their first hesitant steps in the relationship. Francis is embarrassed because his palm is always wet. Nicole pretends she enjoys the cowboy films. Their love is coloured by the romanticism of films and books, presented in glowing technicolour moments: Nicole coming into view through the haze of heat as they wait for Larry's homecoming, Francis promising he will buy her a beautiful dress one day, his moving and ironic declaration that he will never leave her.

The romantic tenderness is shattered by Larry's action and Francis's inaction, to be replaced by anger and bitterness. Francis hangs on to a romantic dream that Nicole could maybe still be his girl, and tells us that this is the one thing that could possibly change his mind about killing himself, but he has to accept that this will never be. The final scene between him and Nicole establishes that their relationship is over.

Comradeship

A bond is formed between the soldiers who face death together every day. After the war, while waiting to fall asleep, Francis recites the names of the men in his platoon, calling up their first names, their surnames and their nicknames. This habit is a compulsion he would rather not have, but he cannot forget his companions and what happened to them.

There is comradeship between the men of Frenchtown who fought in the war. They while away the days in the St Jude Club — drinking, reminiscing about old times, teasing each other, listening to each other's plans for their postwar lives. They also acknowledge each other's pain, both mental and physical. When Arthur is drunk and distressed about what the war was really like, Armand, Joe and Francis show him care and compassion.

Neighbourliness

Mrs Belander shows Francis the kind of neighbourly love that is expressed in thoughtful deeds. When Francis first rents the room, she makes him black bean soup to help his cold, assuming that is the reason for his nostrils running, and she gives him an extra blanket. She was also kind to Francis when he was a child, paying him generously for running errands and baking him a birthday cake.

Tainted love

Larry says 'We love the thing that makes us evil' (page 76). The dark side of love and desire is presented through Larry.

Loss

The novel is permeated with a sense of loss, which is linked with the theme of identity. We see instances of physical loss, the most striking and dramatic being the loss of Francis's face. His physical identity has changed, and the change is compounded through his disguise. The former Francis, a familiar sight around the neighbourhood, has been transformed into an unrecognisable figure with his face shrouded in its cap, bandage and scarf and his body draped in an army fatigue jacket. His injuries cause a shift not only in his appearance and in his own sense of himself, but also in the way other people view him. He has become an object of pity or curiosity. People look away or cross the street when they see him coming. In Mrs Belander's words, he is a 'Poor boy' (page 3).

Nicole is physically lost to him. She and her family have left town and he does not know where she is or if he will ever see her again. The knowledge that they 'Left Frenchtown without telling anybody' (page 15) creates mystery and suspense. The description of Francis's visit to their old house in Chapter 3 is shot through with poignancy. He sees a child's face at the window, 'like the ghost of the little girl Nicole once had been' (page 13). He mourns the loss not just of Nicole's presence in the house but of her childhood youth and innocence. The child disappears just as Nicole has, and Francis wonders if it has been a momentary hallucination. The apparition of a ghost-like child is familiar from horror and super-natural stories and films. The neighbour's doleful reply to his enquiry about the Renards' whereabouts — 'All gone…All gone' — echoes in his mind with haunting repetition, emphasising the sense of loss. The new nameplate where the Renards' plate used to be is a tangible sign of their departure.

When Francis does eventually find Nicole, she is changed. What happened at the Wreck Centre, and the events of the last three years, have had an irrevocable effect. The old Nicole is lost for ever.

Appearance, reality and identity

The theme of appearance and reality is closely linked with the idea of identity. Cormier explores ideas of identity and disguise through the characters and the concepts that the novel addresses.

Hidden identity

Francis hides his identity from others and from himself. He does not want to face up to and accept the events that have made him the person he is. He adopts the persona of the avenger with a clearcut purpose in life.

Although Francis's disguise is effective, Arthur recognises him. However, the Francis whom Arthur recognises is the hero, the aspect of Francis's person to which

Arthur can relate. The first person to whom Francis reveals his identity is Larry. His announcement 'Francis, Francis Cassavant' (page 73) serves both as information and as a challenge. As he makes further announcements of his name, to Sister Mathilde and Nicole, we feel him gradually becoming himself.

Francis does not completely obliterate his old self. The identity he assumes as his disguise when he returns to Frenchtown contains a mixture of lies and near-truths. Although he gives a false name, it is made up of genuine family names: Raymond, the brother who lived for so few hours, and Beaumont, his mother's maiden name. He says his parents are in Canada, which is in fact where his Uncle Louis is. He says Norman Rocheleau, who is a genuine Frenchtown young man, recommended the town as a nice place to live. Francis's choice to include some truth is partly a good strategic move — it is said to be easier to lie if you do not stray too far from the truth — and partly perhaps a subconscious acknowledgement of the past and what has formed him, the very things he is reluctant to confront and accept.

Appearance and reality

In Francis's dreams, the boundaries between imaginary and real events are blurred. He recalls the German soldiers he killed, remembering how he shot them with his automatic rifle, the head of one exploding 'like a ripe tomato' (page 19), the body of the other being cut in half. Then Francis tells us these details are not accurate — the soldiers did not die in this way and there was no exploding head.

How people present themselves and the reality beneath can be similarly blurred. Cormier indicates the difference between Larry's glamorous appeal and the reality that lies beneath it, but the qualities that make Larry glamorous are themselves real. The attractive veneer is underpinned by genuine care for the students he leads and coaches.

When Larry tells Francis he would have fallen on the grenade anyway, Francis bitterly reflects that Larry always tried to make him better than he was. He rejects Larry's attempt to improve the reality of what happened, but in the past Larry did in fact make Francis better than he was — as he did with all the students whose skills he developed.

Key point

The themes of novels are the authors' ideas and views on matters that are important to them. The story and the characters in *Heroes* are the compelling means by which Cormier draws us into the world he has created and presents us with ideas about certain aspects of life that interest him.

Guilt, sin, forgiveness and healing

Francis's Catholic upbringing has given him a strong awareness of the doctrines of sin and forgiveness. The habit of praying and ideas about duty are part of his being. He prays for his enemy, he prays as he contemplates suicide, he tells Larry to pray before he kills him. He knows the prayers of his childhood, and he can say the 'Our Father' in French as he was taught by the nuns.

The greatest challenge to his faith comes when he has to acknowledge his 'sin' in not helping Nicole when Larry attacked her. His action, or lack of if, resonates on many levels. He has allowed a dreadful deed to be carried out. He might almost be said to have colluded in Larry's action, or at least have enabled Larry to go unpunished. He has betrayed the girl he loves, let her down at her moment of greatest need. He has let his hero-worship of Larry cloud his awareness of what is right. Now that he realises how deeply flawed his hero is, and how deeply flawed he himself is, the certainties by which he lives are thrown into turmoil and he is filled with guilt. His sins are revealed and 'there was no forgiveness for them' (page 67).

Francis plans to commit suicide — an act that, in the eyes of his faith, is the worst sin of all. When he throws himself on the grenade, his intention is to die. Thwarted in this desire, he intends to kill himself once he has taken revenge on Larry. On the occasion when he climbed up to the church steeple, the main thing preventing him from throwing himself off was the thought of his family. Now, the one thing that might give him the will to live is if Nicole can still be his girl. Francis is steeped in the doctrines of the Church, and debates with himself issues such as how bad it is to tell lies to a nun, but to the end he is prepared to take his own life. This illustrates the depths of his despair.

When he is back in Frenchtown, Francis's face begins to heal. However, his inner wounds are fresh and raw. When he says 'The truth is that I don't care whether I heal or not' (page 55), he is referring to his outer appearance and the importance of hiding his identity, but he could also be referring to his spiritual self. Larry asks him 'Will you heal?' (page 74), and Francis decides not to mention Dr Abrams. However, Larry's question could apply to Francis's psychological damage as well as his disfigurement.

Francis's religion has taught him about the sinfulness of humanity and the need for forgiveness and redemption. However, redemption can only follow repentance, and Larry does not repent. He embraces the deep flaw in his character and attempts to justify it in the name of love.

The church and the convent

The centrality of religion is reflected in the presence of the church and the convent. St Jude's Church is a constant and important presence in the town, and its significance is reflected in the numbers of references to the building in Francis's narrative. When he first returns to Frenchtown, he looks through the kitchen window of Mrs Belander's house and sees the steeple of St Jude's Church. This image is later repeated in a flashback to before the war, when Nicole is talking about what she wants to do in her life while looking at the steeple of the church in the distance. The steeple — a symbol of the church — dominates the sky, an ever-present reminder of the doctrines of sin, confession and forgiveness. Francis climbs the steeple and thinks of ending his life by throwing himself off it.

One of the first things he does on his return is to visit the church to pray and light a candle. Francis's reference to the statue of St Thérèse indicates its position precisely, in the niche next to Father Balthazar's confessional in St Jude's Church. It is as if he keeps the church alive in his mind by recreating the details of its layout. He stands on the front steps of the church with the gun in his bag, waiting for Larry to come back (page 31). The juxtaposition of images here — the righteous authority embodied in the church building and the murderous intention implied by the gun — underlines the tension between sin and forgiveness.

Francis also stands in front of the convent, wondering if its walls hold the answer to what has happened to Nicole. Nicole's association with the nuns and the convent runs through the narrative. The building itself has a 'faded red-brick exterior' and 'black forbidding shutters' (page 80). It is situated next to the school, and the children have to stop their evening games in the schoolyard when the nuns send them scurrying home. Francis's final meeting with Nicole is in another convent, St Anne's Academy.

Text focus

Look carefully at Chapter 14 from 'His voice is a whisper: "Why did you want to die, Francis?"' to 'The desire to avenge what he did to Nicole and to the other young girls, now that I know about them' (pages 75–77). Read it several times.

- The confrontation between Francis and Larry is a climactic point in the story as Francis reveals that he knows what Larry did to Nicole in the Wreck Centre. Their dialogue is taut and dramatic, and focuses on some of the key issues explored in the text.
- Francis tells Larry he wanted to die because he just stood and let Larry rape Nicole. This stark statement carries the weight of all Francis's guilt and his need for forgiveness. Larry's response is to take away the guilt, to tell Francis that he is being too hard on himself, and there was nothing he could have done anyway. This low-key reaction for a moment takes the focus away from what Larry did to Nicole, and highlights what Francis has done to himself.

Larry's disbelief as he says 'You wanted to die because of that?' shows how differently from Francis he perceives the events of that evening. The guilt and self-loathing that haunt Francis illustrate how far he has fallen from his own standards of morality and behaviour. Larry, it seems, has no such moral scale.

➤ The passage refers to different kinds of love. Larry says he loves the young girls who tempt him to sin, and he loves his sin. Francis says all the kids loved Larry. Love is seen as a shifting concept, bearing many interpretations. If Larry's love is misplaced, the same may be said of the love that the young people showered on him — an unworthy and flawed recipient.

➤ The two 'fake heroes' are face to face. Francis reminds Larry that they all idolised him: 'You were our hero, even before you went to war'. Francis's desire for revenge on Larry is inspired not just by what he did to Nicole but by the shattering disillusion Francis has experienced. This disillusion deepens as Larry reveals his desire for 'The sweet young things', and Francis realises other girls have suffered. It gives Francis an added spur to his revenge. He feels 'The desire to avenge what he did to Nicole and to the other young girls'.

➤ The reader feels the 'edge' is not there. Francis is suddenly overwhelmed by the knowledge of what he is about to do. When he tells us he has not planned where he would place the bullet, we feel that the reality of the situation, which has lived for so long in his imagination, will take a different form. His mission will be accomplished in a different way.

Review your learning

(Answers are given on page 82.)

1 Which six main themes are identified in this guide?

2 Which themes are reflected in the following events?

    a Larry's welcome home party

    b The final meeting between Nicole and Francis

    c Francis's visit to the St Jude Club

3 Who makes the following statements about heroism?

    a 'I don't know what a hero is any more.'

    b 'We weren't heroes.'

    c 'Only the Silver Star is for heroism.'

4 Name the three characters most strongly associated with the theme of forgiveness.

5 What different kinds of healing do you find in the book?

Style

➤ **What features does the term 'style' refer to?**
➤ **What is the effect of the first-person narrative?**
➤ **How does Cormier use different sentence structures?**
➤ **How does the use of descriptive detail add to the novel's effect?**
➤ **How does Cormier use settings?**
➤ **How does Cormier use imagery and symbolism?**
➤ **What is the effect of the references to books and films?**

Style refers to the way in which writers present a story. It does not refer to the actual plot, or to the kinds of characters who are described, but to the way in which a writer chooses to tell a story. When you write about style in your exam essay, you need to show that you understand the choices Cormier has made, and you need to discuss and assess their effectiveness.

The list below gives some of the main features covered by the word 'style':

- The point of view from which the story is told. The author chooses a narrative voice — a character through whose eyes we see the story. It may be a third-person ('He took out his gun') or a first-person ('I took out my gun') narrative. Some stories are told from multiple viewpoints, in which different characters give their own accounts.
- The use of tenses — the author may choose to use the past or the present tense, or a mixture of both.
- Sentence structure — the author may choose to use long or short sentences, or just one word.
- Sentences or paragraphs, or any kind of construction that creates a particular effect.
- The importance of setting to the story.
- The kinds of description that are used — the author's choice of adjectives and descriptions.
- The kinds of details included by the author.
- Imagery — the way in which the author uses word pictures.
- Symbolism — the use of a word or image that refers to something more than the surface meaning.

Viewpoint

In *Heroes*, the narrative is told in the first person. The narrator is Francis, and it is his voice through which we experience all the events and characters. The tone of his voice is direct and colloquial, as if the narrator is speaking straight to the reader. Sometimes he addresses the reader, as when he says of Dr Abrams 'Don't take him wrong, please' (page 1). The effect of this is to draw us into a close relationship with Francis.

The whole narrative is presented from Francis's point of view. All his observations and descriptions are filtered through his character, his personality and what matters to him, so we see characters and events in the way that he experiences them. His narrative is influenced by our awareness that his presentation of events in the past is coloured by his knowledge of the whole story, knowledge that he gradually shares with the reader.

Sometimes, his knowledge seeps into his descriptions. For example, he seems to feel straightforward admiration for Larry at first, but some of the language used to describe Larry at the Wreck Centre reveals feelings caused by later events.

Pause for thought

How different would the book have been if Cormier had chosen to use a third-person narrative?

Sentence structure

Cormier creates dramatic effects through the sentence structure he uses. The first sentence of the novel consists of a long series of clauses linked by the word 'and': 'My name is Francis Joseph Cassavant and I have just returned to Frenchtown in Monument and the war is over and I have no face' (page 1). This structure suggests that each piece of information is a straightforward statement of equal importance, so that the impact of the final clause has a huge emotional and shocking impact.

A different effect is created by the long sentence that describes the celebration when Larry returns on leave from the war:

> We laughed and yelled and stopped at the fountain to drink and splash our faces, then crossed the intersection of Main and West and began to march down Mechanic Street, breaking ranks occasionally to pause and laugh, as if we were all drunk without having taken a sip of liquor. (page 60)

The length of the sentence reflects the excited and buoyant mood of the kids, and carries the reader along with them as they dance through the streets.

Short sentences, such as 'And I had not yet killed anybody' (page 15) and 'The next day, the grenade blows my face away' (page 20) use a few terse words to create drama and tension.

Description

Descriptive details paint a vivid picture of the settings. Francis's room has 'low slanted ceilings' (page 3) and, although it is small, it is scrupulously clean. There is an accumulation of words indicating this: 'windows sparkling, the floor gleaming with wax, the black stove shining with polish' (pages 3–4). The clock on the wall is 'in the shape of a banjo' (page 17), an observation that adds to the realism of the description.

A high degree of reality is created through the use of specific detail, as in the account of the food that Francis buys, soft food like cocoa, bread and strawberry jam, which will not hurt his gums or require chewing. He has 'Campbell's soups in the red and white cans' (page 16). The precise evocation of this product is a familiar picture, rooted in the context of the time.

The names of sweets and candy bars add to the sense of realism: 'My special pleasure was stocking the candy cases with Tootsie Rolls, Butterscotch Bits and the big five-cent candy bars like Baby Ruth and Mr Goodbar' (page 49). Nicole allows Francis to buy her some Milk Duds from the vending machine in the cinema.

Sometimes descriptive detail is linked with a powerful emotional experience. Mrs Belander's kitchen table is covered with 'a red-and-white checked oilcloth like the ones we had at home until the bad times arrived' (page 4). Francis's first sight of it is a moving moment for him.

Our senses of smell, touch and taste are stimulated. We experience the stench of war caused by the soldiers' diarrhoea. We respond to the description of the smell of cooked cabbage that is characteristic of the convent, and clings to the people who spend time there. Through Nicole's remark that it is not a bad smell — and better than Evening in Paris, a cheap perfume available from the drug store — she reveals that she values the selfless devotion of the nuns above the worldliness suggested by the perfume. When Francis finally confronts Larry in his tenement, he smells 'the fragrance of pea soup simmering on the black stove' (pages 72–73). The aroma of the soup becomes sickening, reflecting Francis's disgust with Larry and with himself. When Francis and Nicole kiss for the first time, the taste of a peppermint is transferred from her lips to his. The fresh cool taste suggests the freshness and piquancy of their feelings for each other. When Francis's bandages are removed in the hospital, he enjoys the 'sting of air' (page 54) on his flesh.

Sounds add to the vivid descriptions. We hear 'the chug of engine, blast of horn and hiss of steam' (page 57) as Larry's train pulls in from Boston. Each element of the description echoes the sound and movement of the train pulling in, and conveys the sense of eager anticipation. Sister Mathilde's nun's habit means that her arrival is announced with 'The whisper of starched clothing and the clump of heavy shoes' (page 81).

The horrific episode of Nicole's rape is conveyed through sounds: a moan, a rustle of clothing, a gasp, the needle scratching on the record, a whimper. We experience this event as Francis does, as if we are standing in the hallway with him. Through this series of brief impressions, Cormier creates a tense and realistic scene. It has a harrowing effect in a different way from the violent action of the war descriptions.

Settings

Frenchtown

The author creates a vivid and realistic picture of Francis's home district. The everyday way of life is captured through the matter-of-fact references and descriptions scattered throughout the narrative. Cormier names specific streets: the home of Francis and his parents is on Fifth Street and Mrs Belander's house is on Third Street. Many of the houses are three-storey buildings, occupied by more than one family. Marie LaCroix's family lives on the third floor of the Cassavants' house, Joey LeBlanc's family lives on the first floor, and the room that Francis rents when he returns is on the third floor of Mrs Belander's house. Nicole lives with her parents at 212 Sixth Street on the second floor of a three-storeyed grey house. St Jude's Church is on the corner of Third Street and Mechanic Street. The St Jude Club, the Wreck Centre and St Jude's Parochial School are also on Third Street.

Many of the houses, including those on Fifth Street, are fronted by piazzas or verandas. On the first piazza there are mailboxes, one for each family, each with the occupants' nameplate. Neighbouring families gather on the verandas in the evening, the women knitting and sewing and the men drinking beer and talking about baseball. They are proud of the successful local team, the Frenchtown Tigers, whose past and present players include Francis's father and Marie's older brother. Their crosstown rivals are the West Side Knights. The team plays at Cartier's Field.

We build up a picture of youngsters going to the cinema and paying ten cents for a ticket. They hang out at the drug store and the Wreck Centre. When the boys are 21, they can become members of the St Jude Club, where they drink beer and wine, play pool and poker, and arrange Saturday night dances for their girlfriends.

We gather details of people's daily routines and the services the town has to offer. The Monument Comb Shop is the main place of employment. The production of combs was a huge industry in the area, and we know that Francis's father worked in the Comb Shop until he died of a heart attack on the factory premises. His brother, Francis's Uncle Louis, works there as a yardman, and Nicole's father, Mr Renard, is employed there as well. Groceries are bought from Henault's Market and meat from Mr Molnier the butcher. Eugene Rouleau is the barber, a man with a sharp razor and a tongue to match. You could learn to dance, as Larry LaSalle did, at Madam Toussaint's downtown studio. The local newspapers are the *Monument Times* and the *Wickburg Telegram*.

There are town 'characters', like the bar-tender at the St Jude Club, who is known as the Strangler because he used to wrestle in carnivals and had a strangle-hold that paralysed his opponents. Mr Tardier is known for pinching ladies' bottoms as they pass and Joe Tourraine is known by the title 'Crazy'.

The Wreck Centre

The Wreck Centre is presented as an important place in the life of the town, and it also has a symbolic value. Many of the novel's themes are reflected in what happens here. The Wreck Centre gives Francis a home, somewhere he belongs, a safe place away from the streets and the empty parking lots. His life at home is quiet and solitary, so he goes to the Centre after school and at weekends. Through the Centre, young people have an outlet for their energy and an opportunity to develop their talents and abilities. Francis is not the only teenager to find self-belief and self-confidence at the Wreck Centre.

The place is inseparable from its leader, Larry LaSalle. He provides and organises the activities that occupy the youngsters of the town, and becomes their guide, hero and mentor.

The Centre is also the scene of conflict and destruction. As its nickname suggests, it is the place where lives are wrecked. This is the scene of Larry's rape of Nicole, and where Francis discovers not only the dreadful truth about his hero but has to face his own shameful act as well.

The Plymouth Movie Theatre

The cinema is an important place for the young people in Frenchtown. It is their main source of entertainment. The kids pack into the Saturday afternoon matinees for an afternoon of noisy enjoyment. The programme consists of a cowboy serial and two movies. They also watch the Movietone News, which has an educational value by bringing them details of how the war is progressing in the Pacific and in Africa. The whole town jams in together to watch the newsreel of Larry's heroic deeds.

Wartime settings

The village outside Rouen is presented through a series of impressions. With economy of detail, Cormier paints a picture of ruined houses and streets littered with debris, of shadows, alleyways and doorways, and of an ominous stillness.

Imagery

Many of the images reflect the grim nature of the narrative and the characters' experiences. Brutal imagery conveys the details of Francis's facial injuries. He has 'nostrils like the snout of an animal' (page 54) and his jaw and mouth are 'jammed together as if by invisible clamps' (page 54). Francis describes himself when he returns to Frenchtown: 'I am like the Hunchback of Notre Dame, my face like a gargoyle and the duffel bag like a lump on my back' (page 3). These similes compare his deformed appearance with the title character in Victor Hugo's novel *The Hunchback of Notre Dame* — a misshapen outcast who rings the bells in Notre Dame Cathedral, Paris. This allusion resonates on a number of levels. It reflects Francis's bitter acceptance of his appearance, and is another example of the way that Francis's references to books he has read reveal aspects of his character. In Hugo's novel, when the crowd realises that the Hunchback's appearance is not a mask, they are filled with fear and attack him. The people who see Francis's face in London are shocked and frightened.

Blunt images convey the weight of painful experience. When Nicole is attacked, Francis hears 'a whimpering, like a small animal caught and trapped' (page 63). The image conveys Nicole's helplessness and vulnerability. When Francis realises what has happened to Nicole and all the implications of the incident, he says 'It's amazing that the heart makes no noise when it cracks' (page 64). This image suggests the strength of Francis's despair and misery, as we feel him experience a pain so fierce that it is hard to believe that the sound of his very self being wrenched apart cannot be heard.

In a reminder of the themes of heroism and betrayal, the sound of the pistol shot that kills Larry 'is almost like a ping-pong ball striking the table' (page 79). This image encapsulates the complexity of the relationship between Larry and Francis. When Francis goes to confront Larry, 'The gun is like a tumour' on his thigh (page 72), a dramatic and startling image that suggests the malevolent power of the gun and Francis's purpose.

Minor characters are depicted with equally vivid images. Enrico's laugh is like 'a saw going through wood' (page 6), a simile that captures the harsh grating sound and sets the reader's teeth on edge. The image makes us aware of Enrico's ever-present pain, which he tries to manage through laughing and talking incessantly. Mrs Belander has 'blue veins in her legs bulging like worms beneath her skin' (page 3). The simile reflects Francis's capacity for detached observation.

Poetic imagery

The pared-down prose style is illuminated with moments of poetry, and moments of romantic imagination pierce the sombre reality of the narrative. Nicole is described through images and allusions that reflect Francis's view of her as an exalted being. The description of Nicole dancing evokes her graceful movements as she moved 'like a rare specimen, bird-like and graceful' (page 30). This image elevates Nicole out of the ordinary. She is like a rare or mythical being, occupying a world of her own. Francis describes her dipping and turning 'as if her bones were elastic' (page 39), a simile suggesting the strong flexibility of Nicole's body. Francis refers to 'the cologne like spring flowers that always clung to her' (page 14), a simile that reflects Nicole's youth and freshness.

The grim language of the war scenes is broken with the occasional image of surprising tenderness. Cormier captures a fleeting gentle moment in the war-torn French village with his observation that 'twilight softened the ragged edges of the broken houses' (page 14), a visual picture that evokes the dim light creating shadows to smooth and obscure the picture of devastation. The image also reflects Francis's relaxed mood at this moment as he talks with Norman Rocheleau about the old days.

The two young Germans Francis kills have 'apple cheeks' (page 19). This metaphor contrasts healthy, youthful innocence, signified by their plump rosy cheeks, with the violent and untimely nature of their deaths.

Religious imagery

The narrative is studded with images drawn from Francis's Catholic faith. The doctrines, rituals and ceremonies of the Church are referenced in sensuous imagery that highlights ideas of prayer and forgiveness. The smells of the church building are evoked. The burning wax of the candles and the incense whose fragrance always lingers are 'the odours of forgiveness' (page 5). The metaphor reveals Francis's guilt and his need for redemption. The smell of the ashes when he burns the list of hospitals is 'a damp incense burning for Larry LaSalle's home-coming' (page 55). The juxtaposition of the smell associated with a religious ceremony and Francis's intention to kill Larry emphasises the intensity and almost religious fervour of his mission.

When Francis recites the names of his platoon comrades, it is as if he is saying a prayer. He says their names 'like a litany, the names of the GIs like beads on a rosary' (page 18). A rosary is a string of beads used for prayer. Instead of saying a prayer for each bead, Francis says the name of one of his fellow soldiers.

Symbolism

The scarf

The themes of war and identity are presented in the image of Francis's white silk scarf. The scarf acts as a bandage and a disguise. It is associated with the silk worn by the aviators of the First World War. It is symbolic of the battlefields and trenches of Europe, and serves as a link between the two world wars.

Enrico gave Francis the scarf, which he said he had 'won from an air force fly-boy in a poker game' (page 55). The carefree glamour of the scarf's origin has a romantic aura, seen in Francis's picture of the white silk flowing in the wind behind him. The romantic appeal of this image is enhanced by his observation that in reality the scarf probably does not do this at all. Francis's perception of the scarf as possessing some of the heroic glamour of the aviators of the First World War shows his romantic nature, while at the same time reminding us of his need to be hidden and disguised. The scarf enables Francis to hide his true identity from others and from himself.

It symbolises the veneer that disguises awful truths. In Francis's case, it hides the knowledge of betrayal and the self-hatred that is destroying his soul as much as the grenade destroyed his face. It can also be taken to symbolise the surface charm of Larry, the dazzling attractiveness that hides his darker psyche.

Table tennis

The game of table tennis provides the means for Francis to acquire self-confidence and standing in the eyes of his peers. This development is effected entirely through Larry's manipulation. He is responsible for making the sport prestigious and for turning Francis into a star player. Table tennis comes to be associated with aspects of the relationship between Francis and Larry, with Larry's power over Francis and with Francis's debt of gratitude to the man who handed him the gift of victory in their final game.

The pistol shot when Larry kills himself sounds 'almost like a ping-pong ball striking the table' (page 79). When Francis visits Nicole, he watches some girls play tennis and says 'The ball when it lands doesn't have the sharp sound of a ping-pong ball on a table. Or a gunshot' (page 84). It is as if the sound of the ball on the table becomes the sound of Larry's destruction and Francis's final release from the past.

Guns

The gun that Francis carries on his search for Larry is a constant reminder of his mission. It is the instrument he intends to use to kill Larry. It links his experiences in war with the reason he went to war, and what he feels he must do on his return.

The gun may also be seen as the burden of sin and guilt Francis carries, which becomes bearable only at the end when Larry is dead and Francis has been forgiven by Nicole. Ironically, a gun is the means of Larry's destruction, but it is his own gun and his own hand that bring this about.

Key point

When you write about imagery, try to show how the image is used. A comment about why a particular use of language is effective will be rewarded.

Literary references and influences

Courtly love

Francis's love for Nicole has echoes of a literary tradition known as courtly love, popular in the Middle Ages. The conventions of this genre depicted a man hopelessly in love with a woman whom he humbly adored, seeing himself as her devoted servant, unworthy of her attention and longing to be put out of his misery by a word or glance from his loved one. Significantly, when Francis first sees Nicole he is on his knees, 'like a knight at her feet' (page 8). When Nicole looks at him, it is as if her sword has touched his shoulder, and he makes a pledge to give her his 'love and loyalty for ever' (page 8). According to this convention, the woman initially ignores her suitor, and Nicole — having exchanged one look with Francis — does not give him another glance for the rest of the day.

The unrealistic courtly romance of these references is combined with the detailed portrayal of the everyday circumstances of their meeting. It is a maths lesson, and the chalk that Sister Mathilde is using to illustrate a problem in decimals breaks and falls to the floor. Francis's action in picking up the chalk stems from his less than noble desire to keep in the nun's good books. As Nicole enters the room and he looks up at her, the incident is transformed from an insignificant classroom incident into a moment of high romance.

In the literature of courtly love, the woman often watches her knight fighting or jousting, and may grant him a 'favour', an item such as a glove or a flower, to show her support for his efforts. Sometimes there is the understanding that winning the contest will result in winning the lady. Before Francis and Larry play in the table tennis tournament, Nicole hands the trophy to Francis. When Francis beats Larry, she stands with her 'eyes half-closed as if making herself an offering' and calls him 'My champion' (page 45). Francis is again cast in the role of the humble knight seeking to impress the object of his adoration, Nicole.

Books and writers

Cormier's use of literary references is a feature of his style in *Heroes*. The references help to establish aspects of character and themes. Francis's favourite novel is *A Farewell to Arms* by Ernest Hemingway, a love story with a wartime setting. Francis likes Hemingway because he 'seldom used big three-syllable words' (page 11), a preference reflected in the kind of vocabulary used in *Heroes*. He also likes the books of Jack London, which describe heroic struggles against the environment, and the books of great American writers such as Thomas Wolfe and F. Scott Fitzgerald.

Films

The slow build-up of the inevitable confrontation between Francis and Larry, with its sense of destiny and moral imperative, is reminiscent of the 1952 film *High Noon*. This classic Western stars Gary Cooper as a marshal who has a personal mission to face a deadly enemy returning to town.

The descriptions of Francis's appearance, with his face shrouded in the white scarf and only his eyes visible, calls to mind the film *The Invisible Man*. This film, based on the novel by H. G. Wells, tells the story of a scientist who finds a way of becoming invisible, but in doing so becomes a murderer. The film stars Claude Rains and was released in 1933. The poster advertising it shows his character's face swathed in white bandages. This image, and the concept of invisibility or anonymity leading to or enabling dreadful deeds, is reflected in the characters of Francis and Larry in particular. Another echo of this idea may be seen in the soldiers' uniforms, which in effect render their real selves invisible.

In *Heroes*, Cormier chooses to have Joey LeBlanc die on the beach at Iwo Jima. This detail may have been inspired by the 1949 film *Sands of Iwo Jima*. It features John Wayne, star of countless Western films, as the dedicated, notoriously tough soldier Sergeant Stryker who leads his men into battle and sacrifices his life for his country. Another aspect of the Iwo Jima conflict that is reflected in *Heroes* is the manipulation of appearance and reality. A famous photograph of the US army planting its flag at the summit of Mount Suribachi as a sign of victory was later revealed to have been a set-up. A flag was first planted a couple of hours earlier, but was thought to be too small to be seen from the foot of the mountain.

In *The Invisible Man*, the title character's anonymity allows him to commit murder

US marines raising the flag on Iwo Jima, 1945

Text focus

Look carefully at Chapter 3 from 'I don't want to think about them, those GIs in my platoon' to 'The next day, the grenade blows my face away' (pages 18–20). Read it several times. The description of the battle scene illustrates many of Cormier's stylistic techniques. The incident is described vividly and the action unfolds rather like a scene in a film.

- *Visual impact.* The description is visually compelling. The village is evoked with adjectives: 'abandoned', 'ruined', 'debris-cluttered'. The description of the 'late afternoon shadows' making it hard to see if anyone is waiting for the soldiers creates a sense of tension. The picture of the platoon advancing through the village, rifles ready, is one that is familiar from films and accounts of war. Here, Cormier acknowledges our familiarity with aspects of his subject matter and builds on our expectation of dramatic action. The familiarity is emphasised by Francis referring to the contrast between the unglamorous reality of their experience and presentations of war as heroic: 'not like the war movies at the Plymouth'.

➤ *Use of sounds*. Cormier uses short, blunt words and phrases to describe the sounds that accompany the platoon's advance through the village: 'ragged breathing', 'whistling', 'grunts and hisses and farts', 'artillery shells', 'boom'.

➤ *Use of speech*. The dialogue in this extract is sparse. Only three lines are spoken: 'Jesus', 'What the hell are we doing here, anyway?' and 'Hey, Francis, come on'. The snippets of speech convey their fear and bafflement at the circumstances that have led them to this village in France.

➤ *Length of sentences*. Look at the long sentences in this passage with clauses linked by 'and'. For example:

> We are probably taking the final steps of our lives in this village whose name we don't even know and other villages are waiting ahead of us and Eddie Richards asks of nobody in particular: "What the hell are we doing here, anyway?"

This is followed by a sentence beginning with 'And'. This structure creates a sense of continuous action and draws the reader right into what is happening. Short sentences balance this style, as in Francis's comment that the German soldiers are 'Like me'. Our attention is drawn to these two words, which carry a wealth of meaning as Francis is hit by the impact of what he has done. The short, stark statement that ends the scene builds tension.

Review your learning

(Answers are given on page 82.)

1 From what point of view is the novel written?

2 What is the main setting of the novel?

3 Identify three symbols in the novel.

4 Which writer's influence may be seen in the kind of language used by Cormier in *Heroes*?

Tackling the exam

> What are Assessment Objectives?
> What will you get marks for?
> What will take up your time but gain no marks?
> What are tiers?
> How should you plan and structure your exam essay?
> How should you provide evidence to support your interpretation of the text?
> What will turn a C essay into an A* essay?

Assessment Objectives

The examiner marking your exam essay will be looking for opportunities to give you marks, but will only be able to do so if you succeed in fulfilling the key Assessment Objectives for English literature:

- AO1: Candidates respond to texts critically, sensitively and in detail, selecting suitable ways to convey their response, using textual evidence as appropriate.
- AO2: Candidates explore how language, structure and forms contribute to the meaning of texts, considering different approaches to texts and alternative interpretations.
- AO4: Candidates relate texts to their social, cultural and historical contexts and literary traditions.

How these apply to different exam boards

Both AO1 and AO2 are important for all exam boards. AO3 is not listed here as it applies to English language, not English literature. You are unlikely to be assessed directly for AO4 on *Heroes*, but you will impress the examiner if you show some awareness of the social, cultural and historical contexts and literary traditions that influenced the novel.

Breaking down the Assessment Objectives

AO1

* **Candidates respond to texts critically:** this means you must say what you think of the novel and why. You are being asked to **evaluate** it. Of course, this involves realising that the author has made choices and giving your views on how effective these choices are.
* **sensitively and in detail:** this means you must comment on details in the text and show that you can 'read between the lines'.
* **selecting suitable ways to convey their response:** this means writing an essay that (a) is well organised, and (b) uses an appropriate tone for a formal essay.
* **using textual evidence as appropriate:** this means giving short quotations from the text or referring to details in the text to support your views.

AO2

* **Candidates explore how language, structure and forms contribute to the meaning of texts:** the word 'language' refers to Cormier's use of words. The word 'structure' refers to the overall shape of the novel, as discussed in the Plot and Structure section.
* **considering different approaches to texts:** this asks you to show awareness of the different critical approaches to the novel that are possible.
* **and alternative interpretations:** this requires an awareness that there is no single correct way to interpret the novel. For example, there are different ways of interpreting the ending of *Heroes*.

AO4

* **Candidates relate texts to their social, cultural and historical contexts and literary traditions:** this means showing some understanding of the context in which Cormier wrote the novel, and some understanding of the context in which it is set. Understanding what type of novel *Heroes* is and its place in young people's literature will help to develop your understanding and response. However, if you are studying *Heroes* for AQA, it is not strictly necessary to address AO4.

What you will not get marks for

The Assessment Objectives tell you what you *will* get marks for. It is also important to know what you *will not* get marks for.

* Retelling the story. In examiners' mark schemes, a key feature of the lowest grades is 'retelling the story' — so avoid it!
* Quoting long passages. This will waste time and it will not get you any marks. Quotations in general should not be longer than one or two sentences at a time.

* Identifying figures of speech or other features. You will only get marks if you say why the author has used them and how effective you think they are.
* Giving unsubstantiated opinions. You must support your opinions by reasoned arguments and references to the text.

Higher and foundation tier

You will be entered for the exam at either the foundation or the higher tier.

Foundation tier

Although questions in both tiers require the same skills, and ask you to look at how the author's writing creates particular effects and responses, foundation-tier questions tend to be easier than higher-tier ones. The highest grade you can get at foundation level is a C.

Foundation-tier questions generally give you a number of bullet-point hints to help you answer. It is a good idea to follow these suggestions and use them as the basis for your essay plan.

Below are some examples of foundation-tier type questions.

1 **In what ways is Larry an important character in *Heroes*? You may wish to consider:**
  * **his relationship with Francis**
  * **his relationship with Nicole**
  * **his heroic actions**
  * **how Cormier makes you feel about Larry**
2 **Write about the way Cormier uses (a) the scarf, (b) the gun, (c) table tennis. You may wish to consider for each one:**
  * **how it is used in the story**
  * **what it shows**
  * **why it is important**
3 **How does Cormier present ideas about heroes? You may wish to consider:**
  * **characters who you think are heroes**
  * **characters who are thought to be heroes but may not be**
  * **how the writer makes you see these characters**

Higher tier

At higher tier you may not be given bullet-point hints to help you. If you are, it is a good idea to use them as the basis for your essay plan. You may find that your question is more sophisticated than those on the foundation-tier paper.

In particular, you may be asked to write about themes or style as well as character. You may be directed to read a particular passage and write about not just the passage itself but how it fits into and reflects aspects of the novel as whole.

Below are some examples of higher-tier type questions.

1 **How does Cormier explore the theme of forgiveness in *Heroes*? You should make detailed reference to character and language in your answer.**
2 **What do you find interesting about the way in which Cormier presents tension in the novel? You may wish to consider:**
   * **the way the narrative is structured**
   * **the use of flashback**
   * **features of language and style**
3 **How important are the settings in *Heroes*?**
4 **Read Chapter 17. Discuss:**
   * **how far you find this a satisfactory ending**
   * **how far the style and language of the chapter are typical of the novel as a whole**
   * **how the way in which this chapter is written affects your response**
5 **What do the minor characters contribute to *Heroes*? In your answer, you should consider what they contribute both to the plot and to the themes.**

The question

Breaking down the question

Read the question carefully several times, and attempt to break it down into parts to work out exactly what you are being asked to do. It is a good idea to underline or circle key words in the question.

Interpreting the question

Sometimes a question is open to different interpretations. If you find the meaning of a question unclear or think it could be taken in different ways, make sure you explain to the examiner how you are interpreting the question and how you intend to answer it.

Key point

Read the question particularly carefully if it looks like one you have already answered. The wording will be different and it will require a different response.

Planning your answers

The form of your plan

Write a brief plan of your answer. You can do this in bullet-point form or as a diagram such as a mind map or flow chart. Note the main points that you will make under headings that relate to the question.

Using an extract

If you are given an extract as the basis of a question, you should refer to it closely but also make points related to the novel as a whole. This kind of question may be worded in different ways, for example:

* How far is the passage typical of Cormier's style?
* Discuss how the presentation of Nicole in this passage affects your view of her in the novel as a whole.

Structuring your essay

Think in terms of your essay having three sections:

1 Beginning (introduction)
2 Middle (development)
3 End (conclusion)

Here are some hints for each section of the essay.

Beginning (introduction)

Do not spend half your essay time on an introduction and then find you have no time to develop and conclude your essay. This is a common mistake. Instead, limit yourself to an opening paragraph of no more than about 100 words. This should:

* refer to the question and give an initial response to it
* show you have understood it
* show how you intend to answer it, hinting at the views you will put forward
* explain your interpretation, if there is more than one possible interpretation

Middle (development)

This part of the essay is in some ways easier than the other two. If you have made a good plan, you know what you are doing by now and can follow your plan, point by point, presenting your argument with appropriate evidence to back it up.

Try to make this part of your essay flow smoothly from point to point, showing how the points connect. Use appropriate link words and phrases. These signpost your ideas, giving the examiner an idea of what is coming next and how it relates to the previous ideas. Try not to begin any two paragraphs in a row with the same word or phrase.

Word/phrase	Ideas it contains
However Yet	An exception is coming: '*However*, Larry does good things as well.' *Yet* can also be used without the comma.
Despite this Nevertheless Nonetheless	Signals an apparent contradiction: '*Despite this*, Francis does not pull the trigger.'
On the other hand	Signals a balanced alternative: '*On the other hand*, it could be argued that...' Useful for showing you realise that different interpretations of the text are valid.
By contrast	Compares two features. A paragraph on Francis being an unidentified hero on his return could be followed by: '*By contrast*, Larry is publicly acclaimed as a hero.'
Similarly	Gives a similar example: '*Similarly*, the gun links Francis's experiences in the war with his reasons for going to war.'
Another example	'*Another example* of foreshadowing is found in the references to the church.'
In addition	Introduces a point making the previous one even stronger. After a paragraph on how Francis views his changed appearance: '*In addition*, his facial injuries bring about a change in the way others respond to him.'
Above all	Introduces the most important of several points: '*Above all*, Francis is single-minded in his mission.'

End (conclusion)

The conclusion should draw your arguments to a logical close, but it should not simply repeat them in a different form.

If you have explored two or more sides of an argument, use the conclusion to state which side you personally take. For example, 'Having looked at both sides of this question, I feel that...'

Your conclusion should, above all, refer back to the question, showing you have not lost sight of it. Try to give an overview of your essay as a whole. You could include a quotation from the text in the conclusion, especially one that refers to the essay question. For example, 'I think that although Larry "had been a fake all along", there are aspects of his character that may be admired and even respected.'

Using quotations and referring to the text

It is essential to use quotations and reference to the text in your exam essay. This is to provide evidence for your argument. You can express your personal views on the text — in fact, the examiner will be delighted to read something original. However, you must always back them up with this kind of evidence.

Separate quotations

The first kind of quotation you can use is the separate quotation. This means making your point, then giving the quotation on a separate line:

Larry is a dazzling dancer:

'He could tap-dance with machine gun speed and make daring leaps across the stage.'

Embedded quotations

An embedded quotation is one that runs on from your own words on the same line:

The familiarity of the church with its 'smell of burning wax and the fragrance of old incense' is vividly evoked.

Referring to the text

It is not always necessary to use a quotation. If you cannot accurately recall or find the quotation you want, it is often just as good to refer to it:

When Arthur tells Francis that he has earned the right not to talk, he is giving him the consideration due to a hero.

This technique is also useful if you need to sum up a lengthy passage:

Nicole reveals that she is finally getting better when she tells Francis that for a long time the Monument postmark on Marie's letters gave her the shivers and she tore the letters up. Now she is able to read the letters and can even write back.

Writing in an appropriate style

Remember that you are expected to write in an appropriate style for a formal exam essay. You must write in an appropriate **register**. This means:

* not using colloquial language or slang (except when quoting dialogue): 'Francis blows away the German soldiers.'
* not becoming too personal: 'I can really relate to how isolated Nicole feels because I have felt there is no one I can tell things to.'
* using suitable phrases for an academic essay. For example, it is better to say 'It could be argued that...' than 'I reckon that...'
* using the word 'I' sparingly — it can be effective to use the first person in the opening and closing paragraphs, where you state your intentions and then give your considered opinion

Sample essays

Four sample essays are provided below — grade C and grade A* answers to two different types of questions: a character-based question and a theme-based question. Try reading the grade C essays first and see how you could improve on them. Then read the A* essays. Remember that there could be many different good approaches to the same essay. These sample essays are not meant to be learned by heart and reproduced in the exam.

Question 1

'Now I'm starting to find out what I am, who I really am...' To what extent do the main characters in *Heroes* learn about themselves in the course of the novel?

Grade C essay

1 Focuses on the question. Poorly worded. Limited view

The main characters are Francis, Larry and Nicole. They all learn a bit about how they react to new experiences and in different circumstances. The two men find out about what they are like in war, which is like a testing ground, and Nicole finds out what it's like to get raped.[1]

2 Inappropriate language

3 A sound point but not developed, and some inaccuracy

Francis has lots of new experiences in the book. He has never had a girlfriend and then Nicole comes along and he really fancies her.[2] He finds out how much he can like someone, although she doesn't take much notice of him at first and even waves at Joey right in front of him.[3] Francis also learns that he can be good at something when Larry teaches him table tennis. This does him a lot of good.

Larry sets up a 'doubleheader', that is a table tennis tournament and a production for the same weekend. Larry is scheduled to play in the afternoon and Nicole tells him she really wants him to win. Francis wins all the games, including the final against Louis Arabelle, and then he beats Larry as well, although Larry lets him.[4]

4 Makes the point but slips into irrelevant narration

Francis learns that he doesn't do what he says he will. He says he will look out for Nicole, but when Larry attacks her he doesn't do anything. He feels guilty and wants to die, so he lies about his age and signs up for the army. He learns about himself during the war. He finds out what it's like to kill someone:

5 Quotation not well chosen

'In the alley that day, I encountered the German soldiers, all right, but my bursts of gunfire killed the soldiers quickly.'[5]

6 Good points but insufficiently developed

He learns about comradeship in the army, and remembers the names of all those in his platoon.[6]

Francis finds out what it is like to have no face. His got blown away when he fell on a grenade because he wanted to die. He discovers how he feels when people are scared of his appearance and realises that he feels bitter about it.

Francis also learns that he is capable of killing someone, which he does when he is in the war. He does not actually kill Larry, and Larry doesn't think Francis could have done it in cold blood. We don't know, because Francis got out of it because Larry said he would do it for him.

7 Good points and quotation, but wanders off the point. Poorly expressed

Nicole finds out that she likes the attention that Larry gives her. She says 'he made me feel special'. She seems to think quite a lot of herself when Larry makes her the star of the show and all that. She seems a bit snooty because she keeps herself to herself apart from Marie. [7] When Larry goes to war and the Wreck Centre closes, she spends more time with Francis and they start to date. Nicole finds that she likes him.

The biggest thing that Nicole finds out about herself is that she can survive something dreadful because at the end she is getting better. She comes across as quite strong.

8 Another good point but weakly expressed. It is not a good idea to end with an example

I don't think Larry finds out a lot about himself because, in a way, he knew it all already. He knows what he is like and what he has to do is keep it from other people. He is so used to being what he is that he is almost surprised when he's questioned about it, like by Francis at the end.[8]

Grade A* essay

1 Strong introduction
— refers to the
question and gives
an opinion that will
be developed

Nicole makes this statement at the end of the book, which implies that up until this point she has not developed full self-knowledge. Francis, on the other hand, has had to learn new aspects of himself, and go through a painful process of growth before he is able to accept himself. Larry, it may be said, is different from these two characters. He has always had self-knowledge and learns little or nothing new about himself throughout the novel.[1]

2 Good textual
references — shows
an awareness of the
author's manipulation
of point of view

Nicole is presented as a young girl with the capacity to have fun and to enjoy life. She has a 'hint of mischief' in her eyes, and we see her laughing and giggling with her friend Marie. She seems aware of Francis's interest in her, and there is a teasing note in her voice when she speaks to him. Although she is associated with the nuns and the convent, and seems close to Sister Mathilde, she is not seen by the reader as a holy or spiritual character. The pure and saintly characteristics that are attributed to her reflect Francis's perception, and his descriptions of Nicole perhaps say more about Francis than they do about her.[2]

3 Maintains focus
on the question

In fact, in many ways Nicole seems to be a more worldly person than Francis realises. She is new to Frenchtown, coming 'all the way from Albany, New York', which makes her a little different and places her outside the familiar network of neighbourhood families. She seems perhaps more sophisticated than the other girls. At the Wreck Centre, she keeps her distance from them, and her talent as a trained dancer also sets her apart. At the end of the book, she realises that Larry tapped into her desire to dance and be a star: 'Made me think that I was a ballerina.'[3] She realises that her head was turned by Larry's attentions, that she was flattered by his admiration and dazzled by the show-biz aura Larry brought to the Wreck production.

Larry's departure for the war leaves Nicole free to discover other aspects of her personality. She enjoys her relationship with Francis, and talking about her hopes and ambitions for the future. She discovers a more serious side to herself, spending time with the nuns in the convent and becoming a volunteer with the Red Cross.

In her final meeting with Francis, Nicole emerges as a strong character, perhaps strengthened by her dreadful ordeal. She is planning for her future, thinking that she may become an English teacher. She shows Francis affection and compassion, and encourages him to write. Without realising how much it is needed, she is giving him hope for the future. However, she knows what he is reluctant to face — that there is no future for the two of them — and she takes the sad responsibility for giving him this answer.

It seems as if Nicole's ordeal forces her into a painful growing up.[4] She can assess how damaged she is, how far she is 'adjusting'. Her maturity is sharpened by her anger, as she says 'Don't I look as if I'm all right?', and softened by her humour, when she says that Marie LaCroix should liven up any convent. In the end, Nicole discovers she is strong enough to survive.

Francis also has a painful journey to self-knowledge.[5] His persona as the solitary, bookish boy, with no talent in any area that matters, is developed through Larry's intervention, and he gains status by becoming the table tennis champion. Years later, after the war, Arthur says 'You were the champ there', illustrating how this achievement brought Francis into the public eye and gave him a place in the town's folklore. However, Francis knows that the ultimate championship has not been fairly won but is a gift from Larry — a gift he is grateful to accept. Francis knows he is not what he seems, but at this point he is happy to present a false identity.

Francis discovers that he is unable to stand up to Larry. He wants to stay at the Wreck Centre that night, but cannot withstand Larry's insistence that he must leave. Then, when he knows what is going on, he does nothing. This must be the moment of Francis's worst discovery about himself, the knowledge that he so shamefully betrayed the girl he loved. His self-awareness and self-loathing cut so deeply that he wants to kill himself, a feat he fails to manage on two occasions: once when he climbs up to the church steeple, and once when he throws himself on the grenade. All his energy from this point is channelled into finding Larry, a quest that takes him over and in a way prevents his growth and development. Francis closes every door to the future, destroying the details of Dr Abrams and Enrico. Far from growing in self-knowledge, he blocks out awareness of anything other than his self-imposed mission. The scarf and bandage hide his face, his outer identity and his inner identity. Francis will not know himself until he reaches the point of confrontation with Larry.[6]

4 Maintains the argument

5 Good link between paragraphs — moves on the argument

6 Perceptive point and good focus on the question. Analysis of the author's presentation

At the end of the book, Francis is ready to explore the idea of a future. He has learnt that he is capable of shameful deeds. The old certainties have been challenged — as he says, 'I don't know what a hero is any more.' He will be enabled to live with his self-knowledge by his recognition and experience of forgiveness.

7 Maintains focus on the argument

In contrast, Larry does not learn about himself. We see in his character examples of a multi-faceted persona, but no real change.[7] He may surprise the reader — for example, in his eagerness to sign up when war is declared, and in his subsequent heroism — but there is no indication that Larry finds out about himself from these experiences. He is not troubled by self-doubt. He accepts the dark flaw in his character, and sees no reason to try to overcome it. 'I love the sweet young things' he tells Francis, and asks if that one fault in him wipes away all the good things he has done. Larry's suicide is not prompted by an awareness of the damage he has caused and the lives he has ruined, but by the knowledge that his life as he knew it is over now that he is physically and psychologically damaged by the war.

8 Refers to the question and gives personal opinion while avoiding simple repetition

The characters who grow and find out about themselves are the ones we admire. There is something heroic about the way that Nicole and Francis deal with and face up to self-knowledge. They discover, and will continue to discover and explore, their real identities. Larry's failure to develop different attitudes to his own needs and desires consolidates him as a false hero whose moral blindness we condemn.[8]

Question 2

What does the wartime setting contribute to the themes and ideas in *Heroes*?

Grade C essay

1 Refers to the question, but this is not a strong introduction. Does not preview what is to follow

The wartime setting is important. Everything, or nearly everything, happens in wartime because the USA comes into the war in the course of the story when Pearl Harbor is attacked, and at the end it has finished because all the men are back in Frenchtown.[1]

What happened to Francis shows us the effects of war. He hasn't got any face and his ears are 'just bits of dangling flesh'. His nostrils are like little caves and they run all the time. He has to wear dentures. He covers his face with a bandage and a white silk scarf.

2 Presents a basic
point with some
irrelevant detail and
repetition. Looks at
how effects are
achieved

His friend Enrico, who he met in hospital, has been injured as well and he hasn't got any legs. Enrico is quite funny and bitter and he talks a lot. Cormier describes very well the pain of his injuries. Enrico claws the air where his legs were. Francis's nose runs all the time and the phlegm runs down his throat, making him choke and cough.[2]

One of the themes in the book is heroes. It shows heroes in war who may not be real heroes:[3]

3 Identifies the theme
but does not develop
the discussion.
Quotation does not
support the point

'In the alley that day, I encountered the German soldiers, all right, but my bursts of gunfire killed the soldiers quickly, no exploding head, no body cut in two, although one of them cried *Mama* as he fell.'

This shows partly what really happened and partly what is just a bad dream, which is another effect of war. Francis is a hero, though, because he falls on a grenade and has his face blown away. His action saves the lives of lots of men so he gets the Silver Star. He thinks he does not deserve this and doesn't think he is a real hero. Everyone else thinks he is. He thinks he isn't a hero because he wanted to die.

The other person who is a war hero is Larry. He gets the Silver Star as well, for saving the lives of a whole platoon by capturing an enemy machine-gun nest. Everyone in Frenchtown sees him on the newsreel at the Plymouth movie house.

'He was unshaven, face gaunt and drawn, eyes sunk deep into their sockets.'

4 A good point but
does not focus on it.
Some irrelevance

This shows another effect of war, that Larry doesn't look as good as he did. Larry seems to be a bigger hero than Francis because he gets national recognition and is called 'one of the great heroes of Pacific action'.[4] A lot of the American action in the Second World War took place in the Pacific. Francis's action was in France.

5 Repetition without
development

Larry gets a lot of recognition when he comes home on leave. The mayor and everyone meets him when he gets off the train. He has 'ribbons and medals' on his chest, showing what a hero he is. There is a description of him with his rifle and bayonet pumping bullets into the enemy. This shows him in action, which is why he is a hero.[5]

When he is home on leave, Larry rapes Nicole. This shows that he is not such a great hero after all. He doesn't agree with this and

6 A good point but
not well expressed or
developed

thinks his one sin shouldn't cancel out the good. This is one of the themes that the war bits help to show.[6]

What the war also shows us is that you cannot go by appearances, which is another theme of the book. Larry appears to be a good hero and everyone in Frenchtown looks up to him, but the reality is a bit different. Francis's appearance hides what he is and helps him to keep up a disguise so that he can stalk Larry.[7]

7 A good point but
needs development

Grade A* essay

1 Focused beginning
that shows under-
standing of the
question. Indicates
the approach that
will be taken

The wartime setting is inextricably linked to many of the ideas that Cormier develops through the characters and plot of *Heroes*. The war provides a means through which concepts of what it is to be a hero are explored, and questions about behaviour and intention are raised. The experience of war changes aspects of characters' identities and alters their lives. The extraordinary circumstances of fighting a world war present a testing ground for all kinds of people to come face to face with concepts of bravery, loyalty, comradeship, and national and community spirit.[1]

2 Good reference
and use of quotation

Francis is acclaimed as a war hero because his action in throwing himself on a grenade saved the lives of many men. He is awarded the Silver Star medal. As the bartender says, there are many medals for outstanding service but 'only the Silver Star is for heroism.'[2] In wartime action, outstandingly brave behaviour is honoured and valued. We see this in the deep respect given to the holders of the Silver Star award. In the St Jude's Club the veterans drink a solemn toast to the men who wear the medal, and Arthur questions Francis in awe: 'How many men were you willing to die for?'

3 A good point,
showing how Francis
and Larry are similar

Larry, too, gains the Silver Star for heroic behaviour 'in the steaming jungles of Guadalcanal in the South Pacific'. His actions are feted on newsreels and radio broadcasts. When he returns home on leave, the town gives him a civic reception and celebrates their first big war hero. The behaviour in war of both Francis and Larry demonstrates courage and a willingness to give your own life for the greater good or for the lives of others, attributes that are deemed heroic.[3]

However, Francis is reluctant to accept that he is a hero. In the first chapter, he turns away in disgust when Enrico refers to his Silver Star, and at the end of the book he tells Larry 'I'm not a hero'.

4 Confident analysis of presentation of theme. Shows analytical response to the author's method, and shows how the war setting enables a comparison of Francis and Larry

Francis thinks he does not deserve his medal because when he threw himself on the grenade his intention was to kill himself. He had no thought of saving other lives. He is a reluctant hero whose injuries enable him to hide his identity and not face the public's acclamation. Larry's face, on the other hand, fills the screen at the cinema, and he accepts the town's adulation. Through the contrast between Francis and Larry, Cormier focuses on the tensions between behaviour and intention, and the contrasts between people's moral nature and their actions.[4]

Francis's insistence that he is not a hero may be conditioned not only by his motives for falling on the grenade but also by the knowledge that in a non-war situation — when he did not intervene to help Nicole — his actions were definitely not heroic. However, in looking for a chance to die, Francis saved his patrol. Cormier raises the question: can an action be heroic even if the intention that spurs it is not? In the same way, through Larry's question 'Does that one sin of mine wipe away all the good things?', the author asks us to consider if a corrupt person can do an honourable deed. Cormier does not provide an easy answer to these questions, but makes the reader aware of the ethical ambiguities in human behaviour.[5]

5 Develops the argument, showing how the war setting enables Cormier to present a philosophical question

6 Refers back to the question

Cormier's choice of a wartime setting[6] enables him to raise further ideas about the nature of heroism. The descriptions of how frightened the soldiers were, how they were just scared boys in uniform, far from home, stinking and vomiting, 'nobody displaying heroics or bravado', make us aware of the reality of war, and at the same time provide another view of heroism. As Francis says at the end of the book, the ones 'who stayed, did not run away, fought the good war' are the real heroes. Among these men are those in his old platoon, who are honoured not with medals but in the way that Francis remembers and recites their names, as in Chapters 3 and 17.[7] The real heroes include Arthur and the others, who stuck it out and came home with their legacies of war: Arthur's twitching mouth and mournful drunkenness, Armand's flashes of terror, George's missing arm, Enrico's missing legs.

7 Valid use of textual reference without quoting from the book

Heroes does not only illustrate the destructive effects of war, it gives us an insight into the way that in testing times of national crisis people bond together and discover their strengths as well as their weaknesses. We see comradeship among the men, not only during the fighting but after their return, in their companionable

8 Good use of short quotes to demonstrate style

banter in the club and in the way that Armand and Joe take care of Arthur when he is drunk. Armand's murmur 'Poor Arthur' echoes Mrs Belander's 'Poor boy' as she studies Francis's scarf and bandage.[8] An effect of the war is to arouse compassion and fellow feeling.

9 A perceptive point, demonstrating an overview of the novel and the essay question

Cormier also uses the war to illustrate the importance of community.[9] The war brings out a sense of shared purpose and a town pulling together. People fill the gaps in jobs left vacant by those who have gone to fight and the factories go on 24-hour schedules to manufacture goods needed by the services. The nuns knit socks and scarves for the forces. Nicole helps them, then becomes a volunteer with the Red Cross. The city is dark, with the streetlights dim and windows blacked-out, and the town observes holidays quietly with no bonfires, parades or fireworks. The reader feels the war is being fought not just by the armed forces.

10 A good conclusion that refers back to question, which shows an awareness of the author's choices and makes a supported final assessment without repetition

The wartime setting is a dramatic backdrop to the story. It might be argued that Cormier could have explored the themes of the novel in many different settings, but his choice of the Second World War and how it affects the characters and the town helps to create a resonant and compelling narrative. The images and pictures created by the war, such as Francis's face wrapped in the scarf and bandage, the village in France, and Larry's triumphant homecoming, provide a powerful vehicle for the novel's themes and ideas.[10]

Review your learning

(Answers are given on page 82.)

1 What four things should you avoid because they waste time and earn no marks?
2 What are the two ways to use quotations?
3 What other kind of textual evidence can you provide?
4 What should you do to the question before attempting to answer it?
5 What should your introduction and conclusion ideally mention?
6 What does 'writing in an appropriate style' mean?

Answers

Answers to 'Review your learning' questions.

Context (page 6)

1 Cormier uses his own home district, French Hill, as the basis for Frenchtown, where *Heroes* is set. His interest in films and literature is reflected in the novel.
2 This is the week when the American Library Association publishes the list of books that people have claimed to be unsuitable for inclusion in public libraries or the school curriculum.
3 Pearl Harbor was attacked on 7 December 1941.
4 Franklin D. Roosevelt was president when the war began, and Harry S. Truman when it ended.
5 The US public was angry and determined to fight. A feeling of patriotism swept the country and many thousands of people rushed to join the armed forces.

Plot and structure (page 27)

1 The cinema is called the Plymouth.
2 The full name is St Jude's Parochial School.
3 Larry's last musical production at the Wreck Centre is called *Follies and Fancies*.
4 The novel begins in March and finishes in April.
5 Francis lives with his Uncle Louis after his father dies.
6 The Japanese attack on Pearl Harbor causes the after-show party to be cut short.
7 Nicole's family moves back to Albany, New York after leaving Frenchtown.
8 Chapters 2, 7, 9, 11 and 12
9 Chapter 11
10 Chapters 2 and 17

Characterisation (page 42)

1 a Nicole
  b Larry
  c Dr Abrams

    d The bartender, known as the Strangler

    e Sister Martha

 2 **a** Larry to the Wreck Centre youngsters

    b Arthur to Francis

    c Francis to Nicole

    d Francis to Larry

 3 It is a sin; he does not want to disgrace his family; he wants to die a more noble or heroic death.

 4 Fred Astaire

Themes (page 52)

 1 This guide discusses the following themes:
* heroism
* war
* love
* loss
* appearance, reality and identity
* guilt, sin, forgiveness and healing

 2 **a** Heroism; war; appearance, reality and identity

    b Heroism; love; loss; appearance, reality and identity; guilt, sin, forgiveness and healing

    c War; heroism; appearance, reality and identity

 3 **a** Francis

    b Arthur

    c The bartender, known as the Strangler

 4 Francis, Nicole and Larry

 5 The novel focuses on physical, psychological and spiritual healing.

Style (page 64)

 1 The novel is written in the first person, from the point of view of Francis Cassavant.

 2 The main setting is Frenchtown, Monument.

 3 Three symbols are the scarf, table tennis and guns.

 4 The influence of Ernest Hemingway may be seen in the kind of language used.

Tackling the exam (page 80)

 1 Do not:
* retell the story
* quote long passages

     * identify figures of speech without discussing their effectiveness

     * give unsubstantiated opinions

2 Quotations can be separate or embedded (run on from your own words).

3 References to events or passages that you do not quote directly.

4 Break it down and consider whether there are different ways to interpret it.

5 The introduction and conclusion should mention the question.

6 Writing in a fairly formal way, without colloquial language or slang.